FROM A
BLACK
PERSPECTIVE:
THE BLOOD

Curated & Edited by Rainbow Room Publishing, LLC
Foreword by James Earl Hardy
Cover Art: "Abolition" from the collection "Witness" by Senyah Haynes

FROM A
BLACK
PERSPECTIVE:
THE BLOOD

RAINBOW ROOM PUBLISHING
www.rainbowroompublishing.com

Table of Contents

Acknowledgements x

FOREWORD...xiii
By James Earl Hardy

SCOT FREE...1
By Eddie S Pierce Jr

TRANSITIONS...11
By Senyah Haynes

UNFEIGNED ADORATION...47
By Katrina Harvey

SYNTHESIS...61
By Donell Bonaparte

GRAFFITI PARK...73
By Ken Compton

IN THE COMPANY OF WOMEN...107
By Crystal Renée

ACKNOWLEDGEMENTS

To the Contributing Authors,

My most heartfelt gratitude to you for entrusting me with the literary representation of your blood, sweat, and tears. Your contribution to this project renewed my faith and devotion to the pursuit of my literary dreams. Our collaborative efforts have refueled my passion for writing and the promotion of aspiring and published authors. I eagerly look forward to the positive impact this work will have on our community and the conversations it will inspire in the world as new literary voices emerge.

To Brother James Earl Hardy,

Thank you for nearly ten years of mentorship in both the art and the business of writing. The literary trail you've blazed continues to educate and inspire countless aspiring authors. Thank you for lending your talents to this work and for assisting Rainbow Room Publishing as we introduce these new, dynamic and fresh voices to the literary community and to the world.

Eddie S. Pierce
Founder & Publisher
Rainbow Room Publishing, LLC

JAMES EARL HARDY

James Earl Hardy is the author of the bestselling novel *B-Boy Blues*, praised as the first gay hip hop love story. It recently celebrated its 25th anniversary and was chosen as one of the Favorite 100 Titles of the 20th Century by the African American Literary Book Club (#88). There are eight titles in the *B-Boy Blues* series including the latest installment, *Men of the House* (an Amazon Top 100 LGBT bestseller). The stage adaptation of *B-Boy* made its premiere during the Downtown Urban Theater Festival in New York in 2013, leading to a national tour (Philadelphia, Washington, D.C., Atlanta, Oakland) and its official Off-Broadway debut at Playwrights Horizons (every show was sold out). The film version of *B-Boy Blues* wrapped production in November 2020. Mr. Hardy was born, raised and still resides in New York City.

FOREWORD

Words dance. On the page, and off.

They tap and tumble.

They slide and glide.

They twist and twirl.

They bob and break.

They pop and lock.

They bend and bounce.

They shimmy and shake.

They jerk and twerk.

They rock and roll.

They even boogie and oogie.

That's the kind of visual joy I experienced reading *From A Black Perspective: The Blood*. Eddie S. Pierce has assembled an eclectic, inventive posse of wordsmiths for a collection that may be slender in volume but bountiful in pleasure.

In just a few pages, Pierce's juicy "Scot Free" turns the cougar trope— older woman falls for and is duped by a younger man—inside *out*.

Senyah Haynes' "Transitions" is a kaleidoscopic-like portrait, some characters and narratives crisscrossing, where sibling rivalry and racist generational police violence receive vivid shine.

"Unfeigned Adoration" by Katrina Harvey is a telling reminder that the greatest love of all is indeed learning to love yourself—and that one never actually reaches that destination, for there are always new things and new ways to love.

"Synthesis" by Donell Bonaparte is an intensely moving meditation on masculinity, loss, and longing. The emotional interiority that Bonaparte constructs between father and son is palpable and penetrating. No doubt, the novel this excerpt is from, *Walking to Jupiter*, will be a critical and commercial giant.

For crime drama and fantasy fans, there's "Graffiti Park," Ken Compton's wild and whimsically spooky journey involving a detective nicknamed "Sherlumbo" who relies on the mystical powers and guidance of a 300-year-old bag lady to solve crimes.

Finally, for the romantics (and *un*romantics), Crystal Renée documents the intimate entanglements of three female childhood friends—one (somewhat happily) single, one (not-so-happily) engaged, one (unhappily) married—with humor and heart in "In the Company of Women."

My only complaint: this ride ended *way* too soon. So I anxiously anticipate "Volume Two: The People." In the meantime, I'm going to dive right back in and revisit these assured voices that illuminate the tragedy and beauty of humanity with passion and confidence. But this time, I'll pour a glass of white wine and select a soundtrack to accompany each dance…

- James Earl Hardy

EDDIE S. PIERCE

Eddie S. Pierce is a Master's of Fine Arts in Creative Writing degree recipient from Chicago State University, home of the world renowned Gwendolyn Brooks Writing Center. Pierce released his first self-published work, *Love: Something Infinite* and simultaneously launched Rainbow Room Publishing. His second self-published novel, *Love: From Behind,* followed on Sunday June 30, 2013. LOVE Changes, the third novel in the series and the Rainbow Room Publishing Guide are the author's most recent publications both published in 2018. In addition to producing more titles and pursuing numerous other literary and artistic ventures, Pierce is currently overseeing the company's numerous publishing services and expanding the company's offerings in an effort to provide more opportunities for new authors and professionals in the creative arts.

AUTHOR'S NOTE: I'm terribly known for long disclaimers so all I'll say as a matter of introduction that this piece was written in the bygone era during which cellular phones and mobile devices weren't commonplace. We relied on digital clocks in cars, on wrist watches, VCRs, pagers often clipped on our hips or the inside of our front pockets and similar outdated technology.

Hopefully this piece gives you a sense of time and context. Two elements essential when writing virtually any setting. I often dream about where the characters are now and how different things would be given the numerous technological advancements to date. Perhaps I'll provide you an update when I figure it out.

Enjoy.

Scot Free

"You see, officer," Red stammers through the partition separating him from the back of Officer O'Brian's ash white hair, "what had happened was..."

"Oh God," sighs O'Brian, deliberately rolling his eyes toward the squad car dashboard radio. "Here, we go again."
The radio's clock reads 3:45 a.m.

"...me and my girl had just had a fight."

"Really!" says O'Brian forcing his naturally deep baritone voice up an octave while taking a glance in the rearview mirror at the young suspect.

"Yeah, man, I mean, sir. She was trippin' over some ole' silly shit. Shouting, cussing, and throwing shit."

"Well, that could explain her ransacked apartment. So what you do then?"

"I know what you thinking, but I don't hit no females. I ain't nobody's punk!"

"Sounds like you were really angry, son. Where'd you go?"

"Angry! Shit!" Red shouts leaning into the partition, his pecan face now matching his name. "I was on TEN. I grabbed my shit, hit up my boys, and rolled out to the titty bar for some drinks and shit. That's where I was coming from when you picked me up."

"And what time was that again?"

"Man, I don't know. About midnight, but I wasn't even nowhere near nobody's bank the whole night!"

"Didn't you say that your girlfriend works at the credit union?"

"Yes, sir. She been working there for years before we hooked up last year."

"So, you have been to her job before."

"Yeah, but I ain't tryin' to mess up her gig."

"Well, you'd better hope your missing girlfriend turns up safe and sound soon so that she can help establish your alibi. Between your prior offenses, the camera footage, and your prints on the keys, it's not looking too good for you."

*   *   *

"Ten 'til six," thinks Trina, reading the clock at the bank teller's terminal.

"Time to make a move."

She glances with a smirk over to Charlie, the sixty-some odd-year-old security guard, seated by the front door, which displays the hours of operation.

Monday – Friday	**8 a.m. - 5 p.m.**
Saturday	**8 a.m. - 12 p.m.**
Sunday	**Closed**

"Out like a light, as usual. He's about as useful as the temperamental security camera and the alarm system. The downtown branch doesn't have these issues. Just us in the more *urban* areas."

Following a slightly modified version of the routine closing she developed over her past five years as a manager with the credit union, Trina pulls her deposit drawer with one hand while stooping down to grab the two small black trash bags from beneath her desk. She goes into the safe to count out the afternoon deposits. Upon exiting, she secures the door with a reverberating slam loud enough to serve as Charlie's evening wake up call.

"You calling it a night, sweetheart!" shouts Charlie from his seat near the front door.

"Yeah, Charlie," Trina replies, suppressing an accomplished giggle.

She walks halfway to the front.

"I'm heading outback, with the trash," she says, triumphantly raising a bag for him to see. "Should I lock up the rear door as usual?"

"Thanks, sweetheart," Charlie replies with a wave and a yawn.

"I'll be up to check it in a minute."

"No problem. 'Night."

"Same to you, sweetheart."

Trina leaves from the rear, closing the door behind her.

*   *   *

"Attention all units," blares the dispatcher's voice filling the air of O'Brian's squad car. "We have a report of a robbery from North Shore Credit Union estimated time 12:30 a.m. Video footage IDs culprit as a light-skinned African American male, approximately 20-25 years of age, approximately 6'0" in height and 165 lbs. in weight. Dark hair in cornrows…"

"1:49 a.m.," thinks O'Brian staring at his watch. "Looks like we're in for a long night."

"The culprit was last seen wearing a waist-length black leather jacket, dark color baggy jeans, black leather boots, black leather gloves, dark-tinted sunglasses, and a bandana across his face," the disembodied voice of the dispatcher goes on to say. "Units should also be on the lookout for a person of interest, Trina Carson, a middle-aged light-skinned African American female, approximately 5'8" in height and 140 lbs in weight. Brown hair and eyes. Carson is also an employee of North Shore Credit Union, last seen during closing at 6 p.m."

*   *   *

"Did you honestly think I wouldn't find out, Red?!" Trina shouts, throwing a set of keys at his face.

"What the hell are you talking 'bout?!" Red yells in response, catching the keys mid-air.

"I ain't one of those young silly chicken heads you normally mess around with. I know you been cheating on me!"

"Aw shit…"

"Aw, shit is right! You been caught up, nigga."

"Baby, look," Red pleads, crossing the small studio apartment, placing the keys on a night side table.

"Don't pull that *baby* shit with me," Trina replies, avoiding Red's attempt to embrace her. "How in the hell you gone do me like this? I'm around here buying yo clothes, cornrowing yo nappy ass head... You know what, I don't got time for this tonight. It's damn near midnight, and some of us have to be at work in the morning!"

"So we on that shit again! You know it ain't my fault I can't find a job right now."

"Yeah, and I guess it ain't your fault you got a record neither."

"Fuck this shit! I'm going out."

"Know what? That's a good idea. "

Trina goes to her closet. She tosses a black leather jacket, a pair of baggy navy blue jeans, and an empty black trash bag in his general direction.

"And while you at it take yo shit!"

"What the..." he just barely dodges a well-aimed pair of black Timberland boots.

"Fuck you, Trina!"

Red stuffs his clothes and boots into the bag and slams the door behind him.

"Dumb nigga," Trina sighs, her eyes moving intently from the door to the nightstand's keys.

Looking to the clock on her VCR, she sees that it is 11:45 p.m., set an hour later than it is actually is. She rushes back to the closet and pulls out a second leather jacket, a pair of navy blue jeans and another pair of black boots all obviously too large for her 5'8," 140-pound frame. Satisfied with the selection, she assembles another more feminine outfit complete with a short dark brown wig, a non-descript brown short sleeved t-shirt, an ankle length khaki skirt, and large brown framed, tinted sunglasses and lays it all alongside the first.

She goes into the bathroom and takes out a pack of insoles and some small black stuffed garbage bags from under the sink. She opens the last bag and smiles at the sight of several rubber bound 'dead presidents, her passport, and a one-way plane ticket to Puerto Valero on the red-eye, 1:45 a.m.

Finally, she goes to the mirror, takes a comb in one hand, and her long dark brown hair in the other, and begins putting her hair into cornrows...

Footnote:

"According to the Oxford English Dictionary, an archaic definition of 'scot' is 'a tax or tribute paid by a feudal tenant to his or her lord or ruler in proportion to ability to pay; a similar tax paid to a sheriff or bailiff.' Examples of old "scots" include soulscots (which were paid to clergy or church from the estate of a deceased person), Rome-scots (paid to the papacy in pre-Reformation days) and scot-ales (basically mandatory parties with mandatory cover charges).

So in medieval days, to get away scot-free would mean not having to pay taxes or fees, or even at times, the broader definition that we still use today of simply getting away with something without penalty."

Bologna, Caroline. This Is Why We Say 'Scot-Free' (And Not 'Scott Free') By Caroline Bologna for the Huffington Post, December, 14, 2018. https://www.huffpost.com/entry/scot-free-scott-free-donald-trump_n_5c05a550e4b07aec57519c5f

SENYAH HAYNES

Senyah Haynes is also the author of Jayla's Jaunts, a children's book series that chronicles a little girl and her magical aunt as they travel from state to state, learning about Black culture and history. In addition to being a writer, she's an actress, a painter (her work is featured on this book's cover), and a youth development professional.

Pre-pandemic, she traveled as often as possible, and she breathlessly awaits the return of that kind of freedom to wander the world. Subjects she puts a lot of energy into are legacy and serious efforts made toward anti-racism. She works and resides in Chicago and has been a proud south-sider her entire adult life. She'd like to thank the publisher for appreciating her words enough to gather them together in this anthology.

AUTHOR'S NOTE: Transitions is part exercise, part experiment, and part word orgy. As the reader can deduce, way can indefinitely lead to way so no rightful ending truly exists. If you, the reader, are so inclined, do drop a note telling me, the author, which rabbit hole of a vignette would be most interesting to escape further into. Perhaps we can create together. palindromeglobal@gmail.com

TRANSITIONS

There was a spot of blood on the floor that was bothering her. She'd sat in the reclining chair by the wall-to-wall window and stared at it, dried and cracking, as she hugged the blanket with the paltry thread count to her chin in a feeble attempt to keep her body heat close. Behind her, through the window, the sky was aglow with the artificial light coming from every right angle that made up the massive complex of the university hospital where she held post.

Defibrillators. Codes. Rib-cracking compressions in the horror film that had become her life... To think that the events of just a few days before didn't foretell this moment would be possible, that the soothing calm of a storm passed would envelop her. Joyce now had the privilege to have little in life to bother her at the moment but a slight chill and an irksome spot of blood that she would neither clean up herself nor call in housekeeping or a nurse to do. Her aunt, the complete apple of her eye, lay sleeping angelically in the bed next to the spot, oblivious to all but what Joyce hoped were sweet dreams. No longer was she intubated, and during her most recent waking moments, she had no recollection of the death and resuscitation her niece had witnessed that was, in fact, her very own.

It was two A.M., the witching hour, and from the eighth floor of the hospital, the sounds of the city were hauntingly slight. Joyce heard an ambulance cry in the distance, and she craned her neck, then swiveled her whole body in her chair to see it. Fixated, she watched it speed down Cottage Grove Avenue and longed to know that the person inside was going to make it. Days ago, she'd had the same fervent wish, that the person inside the racing ambulance would make it, knowing that person was her aunt. Chasing ambulances was much different from staring at them with a bird's eye view, Joyce thought. Considering that to chase them meant the emergency had hit far too close to home, she definitely preferred to stare.

Her sudden gasp had started deep in her belly and could've sucked all the air out of the room. Next, she cupped her hand over her mouth with the force of a slap, unable to believe her eyes, but subconsciously realizing that waking the sleeping patient wouldn't make this moment any better. The ambulance, which was just about to turn the corner and head for the ER, had swerved to avoid a jaywalker and plowed straight into a pole.

Cleo was dog-ass tired. It was hard enough being homeless, let alone in the wintertime in Chicago. Between the too-thin jacket, the hole in his left shoe, and the heroin coursing through his veins that had long ceased to offer escape but now just fought off sickness, he was fucked up. Living day by day was a distant dream; Cleo was living moment to moment, and as he reached in his pocket, he anticipated with almost childlike delirium the escape the next few moments would hold.

He shuffled along, stumbling in his haze but never falling, and dug deeper in his pocket, searching for his treasure. Damn, not the left pocket; that one was nothing but ripped cotton. He felt himself scratch his leg with filthy nails as his hand passed through the shredded lining. That felt good. He scratched again, harder this time, trying to satisfy an itch that never quite went away. At this point, he wasn't sure anymore if it was the chemical cocktail that served as his blood that made him itch insatiably from the inside or the near-gelatinous coating of grime that glazed his skin like honey on a ham. He hadn't been able to bathe now in ten, no, twelve days. Not since his girl put him out for the last and final time.

Goddamn, he thought, she'd been mad as a bag of bees when she came home to the scene he'd hardly been aware he had set for her. Him nodding out with a needle sticking out of his arm wasn't any kind of novelty and hardly a straw distinguished enough to be the camel's back-breaker. No, he was pretty sure it was the naked woman passed out on the floor next to him, ass sweat seeping into his girl's favorite chenille couch throw cover, that had done the trick. He woke up to the woman, who he'd only really messed around with on an irregular basis and had never brought back home before, screaming and cursing. A large chunk of her hair was vise-gripped in his lady's hand, and she was offering her a physical escort through the front door. Then she ran back to toss out her clothes. Then she ran back for him.

In an undignified encounter of fed-up meeting lost cause, Cleo didn't reach full consciousness until he was walking firmly in the end result, down the street, five blocks from his former home of the last three years, with two black eyes and nothing but the clothes on his back. It was time for another hit.

But that seemed forever ago, and now, as he scratched his left leg nearly to the white meat, he could faintly hear the wail of an ambulance coming closer. There wasn't a soul in sight, and at this hour, traffic was equally as sparse. He'd been shuffling along, seemingly outside of time, down dark sidewalks, in alleys, across the park and wide intersections, all with an equal lack of general regard for anything further than his one foot after the other. He now fished for his treasure again, this time in his right pocket, where he stored his loose change. He found it there, right where he had left it. It was a moment of delight he'd been saving for the right time to maximize its effect, and since he was now walking down the streets that snaked through the university hospital complex, there was plenty of light. And safety.

"I ain't neva…" he said aloud as he unfolded the picture he'd been saving since he'd found it in a garbage can sometime around dusk.

It had been nestled in a heartbreak time capsule, but because Cleo couldn't eat, drink, sell, spend, or shoot up the contents surrounding it, he'd hardly noticed. As he'd sifted through the broken bottle of perfume, the love letters ripped in half, the positive pregnancy test, and the red lace panties (that hadn't been hers), he'd hardly blinked twice. But when he'd come across that photo, the only one that wasn't shredded but simply crumpled up, his enchantment was swift and complete.

Heroin was his escape of chemical need at this point. But his true escape of choice had always been the delicious daydream. As he stepped off the curb, he didn't notice the little red walking man blinking on and off because he didn't bother to look up. Nor did he hear the ambulance siren that had been steadily growing closer until it was a screaming alarm because he didn't bother to listen. All he knew was that at first sight, he'd been swept away on a cotton candy cloud by the image of a life so starkly different from his own, and he'd been waiting for hours for enough light to gaze upon it again.

First, he felt the violent rush of air that blew the photo out of his hand. With that, he was yanked from his inner-most thoughts and could suddenly hear the screech of tires and scream of the siren, its white and red beacons nearly blinding him from their proximity. As the vehicle spun and careened into the light pole, it began to dawn on Cleo that his life had been narrowly spared due to an apparently skilled driver's micro-decision to yank on the wheel, at his or her own peril, as opposed to sending Cleo to meet his maker.

"Shit!" Cleo blurted, standing in the middle of the street where the vehicle should've had free passage.

As the cocktail in his veins added the ingredient of adrenaline, he felt his feet moving before he even realized why. Running at full speed in the direction he had come from, Cleo looked over his shoulder with a twinge of sadness at the photo of that bougie couple he'd left lying in the intersection. Damn, he thought, and he raced across the street and was swallowed by the darkness of the park. The red emergency lights that illuminated the photo were its complete antithesis- there was nothing at all urgent about that image of Sasha and Jerry lying on that hammock near the shark-and-bake shack on that beach in Tobago.

The salt air gave her life. The chorus of sea birds singing their carols and the steady rhythm of the waves lapping on the sand were enough to make her want to change her Christmas traditions forever. What joys were held in a white Christmas, anyway? A blazing sun beaming down a good eighty-five degrees to warm the countless Black bodies beneath it- that was a Christmas worth singing about. And the Black body beside her- now that was more than worthy of hitting a few high notes over.

Sasha nuzzled Jerry's chest, and the hammock swayed gently, contoured to the curves of their bodies like a living piece of modern art. She loved that man like nobody's business, all six-foot-four-inches of him, all 215 pounds of muscle and charm. Like the old Motown song said, if good looks were a minute, then he would be an hour.

He'd proposed just the night before, sticky skin entwined with hers in the heat of Tobago's muggy night after an hour of up-tempo sex. They were actually his final words before she fell asleep, and her only reply had been to drift off to slumber riding the gentle wave of carnal, spiritual, and true heart satisfaction. He'd known her answer before he asked the question. She never had to say it.

And now she was adrift in the bliss of having gained her prize, the gold coin for waiting him out the last five years and enduring what so many other women had, all in the name of love. Denial ain't just a river in Egypt, as they say, and she had crafted a version of their romance that kept her safe in its plot folds. All he needed to do was stay away from the fringes of happily ever-after's expectations, and her version of their romance could carry them the rest of their lives.

But what she didn't know was that she was the whetstone against which he sharpened his collection of psychological blades: narcissism, manipulation, even sadism. She didn't know. She just didn't know.

As for now, on the beach, life was perfect. She gazed at a pair of birds flying off in the distance and saw a complete metaphor for what she imagined was her life to come. Now that she and Jerry would be married, they would move through space and time together, as in synchronized flight, off toward some distant horizon whose unknown character was its sweetest part. The limits to that mystery were as unconstrained as her romantic ideals.

What she didn't know was that just out of her sight, the birds actually diverged. The one that had been slightly in the lead felt the wind on its wing would give better lift if it turned in the opposite direction, and with that change in instinct, without a moment's foreshadow, away it went. The lone bird, so abruptly abandoned, didn't feel the tug at its wing as did the other. It flew a half a mile more on its original course and perched on the fifth level rail of a cruise ship en route to its next Caribbean port. No sooner had the bird's talons firmly closed when a baseball, already airborne and speeding from the cabin toward the open sea, hit it in the head. Before the bird could recognize that anything had changed, its status transitioned from animate to inanimate, and both lifeless objects, having changed each other's trajectories, eventually met the ocean with separate splashes that could hardly be perceived. In the foam of the ship's wake, they both vanished from view, only one of them to ever be, for any period of time, truly missed.

Bobby ran to the rail of the deck, inconsolably sobbing for his squandered ball, and his big brother, Ryan, ran after him. Their mother, who'd not only told him not to bring it, but who had also been chastising their horseplay all morning, was nursing a migraine as she lay in bed with a cold compress over her head.

"I said, stop it!" she yelled, and she rolled on her side and pulled the covers over her head.

Bobby was seven, and Ryan was ten, and the younger was constantly tortured by the elder, today being no exception. Bobby's baseball was the last vestige of his father, who had given it to him on the best day of Bobby's life. The day right before his father died.

It was signed by Babe Ruth and had been passed down for generations from nostalgic father to eager son, but never at such a young age as Bobby. Since his chubby-digit years, he had been fixated on this heirloom, even before he could comprehend the concept of inheritance or understand that his daddy had a daddy, and there was even still a daddy before him to whom it had belonged. In his crawling months, his beeline to the dingy-colored orb resting on its stand in its hallowed place on the bookshelf was inevitable. On all fours, he would stop when he reached the stained wood and gaze up. As a toddler, it was the only furniture in the study that he'd try to climb. In kindergarten, he'd cajoled his father into picking him up to see it at eye level and telling him its origin story for the first time. He'd heard it at least a hundred times since.

And when Bobby was seven, mere months ago, His father had taken it off its stand and said, "Here, Bobby. This ball is yours now."

With less fanfare than had he passed him a morning bowl of oatmeal, he had given his only son- while still a young child- a gift that aficionados had offered him tens of thousands of dollars for. Bobby held it in his hand as though he cupped the Holy Grail - speechless, wide-eyed, ten toes dug into the floor, propping him up. He remembered all the different vantage points from which he'd spied this ball, since before he could form a sentence, and realized that all his life he'd known this would be his most treasured possession one day.

Within twenty-four hours, his father was dead.

This left him feeling discarded in a wilderness of jackals, hyenas, and wolves, all gnawing at his sense of safety and mocking his terrible loneliness. His mother loved him well enough, but as a migraine sufferer, she only experienced either of her children on the periphery of photo-sensitivity, aura sensations, and waves of white-hot pain in her command center over which she truly had no command. Even her grief couldn't penetrate her migraines. Ryan was a damaged child, abused by his biological father, and then neglected by his afflicted mother. For the seven years their paths had been parallel, Ryan's stepfather and he spent courteous and compassionate time together, but the luminescence of the love he showered on Bobby was only a warm glow by the time it reached Ryan, as though light and love had bent and refracted.

And so, with this mixed bag of nothing nice that had equaled the sum of his young life, Ryan's first intense emotion that he could recall was envy. Then he burned with bitterness. Then he experienced hate. And since his stepfather had made his untimely exit from their lives as well as his own, Ryan had exacted the full brunt of his unregulated toxic brew of emotions on his brokenhearted baby brother. The culmination, of course, being when he saw his opportunity to inflict the deepest wound and take something that could've and would've never belonged to him- the Babe Ruth ball.

It was this same ball, whose origin story he too had heard a hundred times, but not while being held lovingly at eye level or while resting in his father's embrace. Usually, he was sitting off in the corner, maybe on the floor or on the step stool, known to be there but really just out of focus. It was that same ball that Bobby had scarcely let out of his sight since his father's death. During school, it was in his backpack. At dinner, it was in his lap. During slumber, it was under his pillow. And when their maternal aunt had generously purchased this cruise vacation for the four of them in hopes of spreading a loving balm on top of their grieving, it had never been a thought in Bobby's mind to leave it.

As Bobby leaned over the rail trying to see his ball that had vanished in the wake, a stab of fear jolted Ryan as he considered that maybe, just maybe he had gone too far this time. Ryan grabbed his little brother and hugged him close, snot, and tears soaking his T-shirt. He'd mastered envy, bitterness, and hate. Now he registered shame as an oddly mature question occurred to him; he thought, why would I want my brother to hurt worse than me?

Bobby, who was bawling louder, broke free of the awkward embrace and sprinted from the deck, through the room, and out the cabin door, slamming it behind him.

"Watch your noise!" his mother yelled, still buried beneath her pillow.

Ryan began to chase after him, but his mother sat upright before he could open the door.

"Stop!" She commanded. "You've done enough. I don't know how to teach you to stop being cruel. Life will have to do that. Now sit down and watch TV."

She burrowed back under her pillow. "And keep the volume low."

Bobby ran up several flights of stairs to the ship's deck, a solace-seeking missile, targeting the only comfort he had left. There he found his aunt sunning, her skin a tan leather that had seen more sunshine than her scant melanin could bear. She had cucumber slices over her eyes and zinc pasted to her nose. With her ear buds firmly planted, she was submerged in the world of her 80's pop, rocking out with her youthful mind decades away from her aging body. She felt a little person snuggle next to her, then curl up and into her side like a lonely fat cat. She didn't need to take the salad fixings from her face; she knew who it was. Bobby was indeed an auntie's boy, always seeking, and receiving the love from her that his mother and her affliction were unable to give him.

Shonda was also basking in the sun, though her melanin-rich skin was well-equipped for every ray cast upon her. She'd only been on the deck about ten minutes, but in that time, she'd gained at least three shades, now glowing like well-polished mahogany. Her sunglasses took up a third of her face, large and concealing in a style reminiscent of the silver screen era of Hollywood leading ladies, shying away from their adoring fans. Through their dark lenses, she saw very clearly, and her eyes watered as she watched the little boy, clearly distraught, come snuggle what must've been his mother. She'd been ruminating on love a lot lately. Actually, it filled ninety percent of her waking thoughts. As she queried back and forth in her mind, which love it hurt more to lose, the love of a child or the love of a mate, she honestly couldn't answer. She knew as a mother, she should easily conclude that the lost love of a child was worse by leaps and bounds, but the fact is they were just different.

The mother, who had cucumbers on her eyes and some glob of white goop on her nose, wrapped her arms around her son without even looking to confirm who it was. It was as though he'd always been en route to her arms, and she'd always had them open and waiting for him, and this moment was a certainty and natural conclusion. The tears ran freely down Shonda's face.

It occurred to Shonda at that moment that she was spying. The glasses she'd worn under the guise of shading her from the sun, but for the real motive of hiding her pain from the world, had offered her this tiny moment where she could watch, unobserved, this tender reminder of the wounds she felt. She remembered when Jontae was that young and how he was such a mama's boy that his main occupation was experiencing the world from behind her apron skirts. If he wasn't in her lap, he was holding on to her leg, or begging for a piggyback ride, or peppering her with kisses while she lay on the couch napping. If ever a boy did love his mama, Jontae was the one, and now Shonda stopped her internal query as she watched the mother and son. Without a doubt, the deepest pain was the lost love of a child.

When Jontae was just a baby, the police had raided their house

from a false tip and ripped her husband from their bed. Screaming,

with her newborn clutched to her bosom, Shonda had watched them

crack her husband's head as they beat him all the way down the stairs

from their bedroom to the front door. She'd never felt that much

terror in her life. With this home invasion so brutal and abrupt, she

could only think to call 911. But of course, with this cacophony of

shouts and commands, guns drawn and pointed at her and her child,

and batons angrily painting the room with fine mists of her husband's

blood spatter, calling 911 would have only brought more of the fury in

blue. In her utter hopelessness, she simultaneously cursed the God that

allowed this to happen, and the society that had no system in place to

protect its citizens by policing the police.

It took more than five eternal hours before she was able to find out that her husband had never made it to the station- that his head had been fractured so badly they ended up taking him directly to the hospital. He was in a coma for three weeks before he silently slipped away one night, as Shonda sat at his side with Jontae suckling at her breast. She would never forget how she had put her head down, how violent her sobs as she showered her baby's hair with her tears. But he had a good latch, and she didn't want to break his suction, so she held him closer as she strangled the sobs in the back of her throat. And they sat like that, nursing and sobbing, her heaving chest spasming with her silent cries like a seismic disturbance. Through the flatline, through the nurses rushing in and the doctor declaring the time of death, and through the chaplain drifting in and fading out, they sat like that. They both held onto each other through desperate embrace and instinctual latch, as they began their journey into fatherlessness and widowhood.

The heartbreak and rage alternated throughout that ordeal. Still, when she found out, against the best efforts of CPD and the City of Chicago, that the warrant and raid were actually meant for the house on their street that was 200 East, not 200 West, her internal blaze was so consuming she wanted to set the world on fire. Those scant four blocks may have started as a careless typographical error, but they amounted to the difference between life and death, hope and despair… wholeness and irreconcilable fracture.

But she was still in disbelief about how lightning could strike her twice in one lifetime. How cosmically cruel that only fifteen years later, her only son would be caught up, riding while Black, and die from bullets coming from the same guns that had been pointed at him and his father all those years before. Wealth and an elite education couldn't save him. Nor could living in a high rise condo downtown miles away from the hood his mother had fled with the settlement money from his father's murder. No amount of assimilation or respectability politics could counterbalance the congenital and historically dangerous condition of existing in this world in the African form.

Shonda took a sip of her margarita and then leaned back in her lounge chair, ripping her gaze from the mother and son. How cruel indeed. Here she sat somewhere in the middle of the Caribbean sea, husbandless, childless, but bathing in the sun, not knowing under the circumstances what else she could possibly do.

Her phone rang, and it was her lawyer. He had called five times before since she'd left the city, and for whatever reason, six was a charm. Shonda took a long sip of her drink, then answered the phone.

"Yes, Bruce. What do you have for me?"

The children were tearing the house to shreds. Sometimes they were regarded as blessings from on high, but at times like these, they were thought of more like the freaks of nature that they really were. The four-year-old identical quads were taking full advantage of their father's distraction. While he was in his office toward the back of their home, they were using the living room furniture as their private jungle gym and screaming like chimpanzees.

"Shonda, I'm so sorry, hold on a second," Bruce stammered into the phone. "Boys, settle down! And stop jumping on your mother's couches!"

As with any other time he was home alone with the children, Bruce would be hoarse by the time he went to sleep that night. In high pitches that rivaled dolphins frolicking as they leapt toward the sun, the boys' squeals passed easily through the walls and drove their father mad.

He hated talking to clients when he was home with the children, but this one had gone AWOL, and communication had been stagnant like a mosquito-infested puddle after a torrential storm.

"Shonda," he repeated, "I'm so sorry, just give me a second."

He placed the phone carefully down on the table and ran into the living room, a wild look of powerlessness on his face.

"Boys, boys, please," he begged.

He'd long since ceded that the traditional roles didn't matter in this parent/child relationship; he was outnumbered and far more suited to arguing in a court of law than corralling unruly children and pleading his case for order in the home.

He began to grab them one by one and place them on separate areas of the couches, sitting them down with such force that each sunk into the cushion and then bounced back up. Eight powder blue eyes looked up at Bruce with dismay, tears welling up in all but one pair. Jarred, the youngest of the four by twenty-nine minutes, had the curious habit of displaying emotions in his brothers' exact opposite direction. Since they were typically a joyful lot, this left him irksomely melancholy most of the time. The child psychologist wasn't sure yet what to make of it. But now, while they were all being chastised by a parentally ill-equipped father at the end of his wits, while his brothers all primed themselves for the waterworks, Jarred burst out in cynical laughter.

It was that laughter that both arrested Bruce's movement and sent a wave of goosebumps shooting up his arms. The exact source of what had startled him, Bruce didn't know. But he was definitely unnerved. His son, his own flesh and blood, the literal runt of the litter... he'd laughed with true cynicism that had no human possibility of forming that completely in just four short years. Was Bruce being mocked? Did the four-year-old think him a fool, a clown, an ass-hat? The sort of brazen imbecile who believes that he can really handle being a first-time parent at the age of fifty-six, all at once to quads, no less?

As the questions collided with one another, the tunnel vision started to narrow. Instinctively, Bruce started his four-square breathing. Four counts for the inhale, hold for four, four counts on the exhale, then hold for four. While he breathed with intention, he counted backward from ten in his head because he could feel his thoughts spinning off uncontrollably. This was a technique his therapist had suggested because his anxiety and paranoid thoughts sometimes broke free of his logic like wild horses on the open plains. He knew all too well what would happen if they remained unbridled too long.

After working the technique and feeling its effects, the tunnel began to widen, and in the light at the end of it he saw his youngest son still laughing like a little Chuckie doll. There were no two ways about it; that kid was creepy.

"Come on, guy… Give your dad a break, why don't you? All I'm asking for is that you boys don't tear the house up while your mom is gone and let me get some work done."

Shit. He'd forgotten Shonda was on the phone. As he ran back to his office, hoping she hadn't hung up, he knew already that she must've. First, she was on a ship in the middle of a Caribbean cruise. This wasn't the most conducive environment to talk business. And though this business was all personal for her, Bruce realized there was really no such thing as good news in this situation. Whether the cop got put under the jail or was given a medal, whether the city awarded her a gazillion dollars or sent her a bill for the price of the bullets they'd discharged into her child, who cared? By now, she certainly didn't. Who and what she'd cared about had been murdered… twice. She was done with all derivatives of that emotion.

The volume on Bruce's phone was turned all the way up, and when he got to his desk, he could hear the dial tone humming steadily. Though he wanted to get her scheduled for her deposition, tell her about the two new witnesses that were going to be subpoenaed, and give her a legal notepad's worth of other updates, he decided instead to pick up the phone and put it back in its cradle. It had already taken him six calls before she picked up the phone the first time. He'd just have to catch her once she was stateside again, he thought, no way he could get her back on the line at this point. That would be as improbable as lightning striking the same place twice.

Instead of diving headfirst back into this civil suit, he decided instead to go play with his kids. They loved it when he was Mr. Wiggles, the alter ego he'd created when they were in their terrible twos. Mr. Wiggles donned the classic horn-rimmed glasses, beak nose, and Groucho mustache combo that Bruce had found in a gag store for five bucks. And once he put that face on, he was a man transformed, no longer shrinking from the weight of his ineffectiveness at fatherhood; Mr. Wiggles allowed him to level the playing field and manage his children through the allure of the next giggles they'd have at his expense if they submitted their attention.

As they rode down the elevator from their twenty-first-floor condominium, he had them on their kiddie leashes. As was his ritual, he gripped the handles for Jarred- yellow and Max- red in his right hand. Zach's blue and Sean's green handles were in his left hand, and his camel-colored soft Italian leather man-purse that his wife had bought him in Milan was crossed fashionably over his chest and resting at his hip.

"Going down!" Mr. Wiggles said in his comic falsetto as he moved his body like his knees were spaghetti.

The boys giggled, Zach more than the others, with his cheeks turning red. He was the easiest child to please. Jarred, of course, pouted and straightened his elbows, jamming his hands deeper in his pockets, as a sign of how closed off he was to this brand of joy. Bruce smiled behind his Groucho mustache; he knew this game well, and when it came to keeping his boys content, his motto was that three out of four ain't bad…

The young woman who got on at the fourteenth floor rushed into the elevator and hovered in the corner with the number panel, pushing the L button in quick frantic bursts as though she were messaging in Morse code. It wasn't until the doors had closed that she was able to absorb her surroundings; eight curious eyes stared up at her in silence. She didn't even notice the father. She was fixated on the colorful leashes tethered to each child. The air felt thin, and she was sure she would swoon if she didn't get out of that car and damn quick. She rubbed her left wrist, wincing at the rawness as she backed against the doors, allowing them to support her full weight.

She wanted to scream but didn't. She bit her lip and let the tears fall while she stood transfixed, unable to tear her gaze from horrid leashes, those tethers that were binding those children. Just moments earlier, she'd freed herself from her own bondage after her rapist had been passed out, dead drunk for a good half hour, and she felt it was safe to actually escape.

By this time, Bruce was oblivious to his own odd appearance and was awkwardly smiling at the woman in the elevator. It certainly was bizarre to face her fellow passengers as she was, and with his boys' unbroken gaze at her quirky behavior, he wasn't quite sure what to say. He did notice the black streaks running down her face. He also noticed she had rubbed her raw wrist and the two broken nails on the hand that had rubbed it.

"Boys, shall we sing the song?" Mr. Wiggles asked in his clownish falsetto.

Three colorful leashes swung back and forth as the boys jumped up and down with excitement. All except Jarred, who stood stoically, staring at the woman. She was startled by his brothers, and a moment later, she nearly fell out of the elevator as the door opened behind her. She caught herself before hitting the ground, and staggering off, she half ran, half limped away. Bruce watched after her for a moment and then led his tiny quartet from the elevator. He allowed himself to wonder fleetingly who she'd been here to visit, as he'd never seen her in the building before. Max's high-pitched laugh jolted Bruce back to the present, and he saw the fading blue of Zach's leash trailing behind him.

"A runaway!" Mr. Wiggles shouted, and the chase was on.

Vero walked briskly from the building's vestibule and frantically flagged down a cab. With a creeping panic, her night played in reverse with vivid frames of everything that had distressed her. First were those kids in the elevator with those stupid kiddie leashes on- Jesus, what kind of fucking parent would do that to their kids- she thought. Then, her race down the hall to the elevator, the way she'd tripped in her haste and skinned her knee on the high traffic carpet though she knew the only one giving chase was a recent bad memory. She remembered how she'd writhed her way from out of the terry cloth housecoat belt that bound her wrists, only beginning her struggle a half-hour after she was certain her client was passed out cold.

Vero had to find another line of work, she thought for the fiftieth time that night. The money she'd been saving as an escort wasn't worth the emotional battery, and now, real physical danger she was finding herself in more and more often. Wentworth McFadden was a millionaire, it's true, and his lavish tastes and equal desire for kink both operated as do most things in the lives of the one percent: in excess and with utter impunity.

He hadn't so much beaten her as he had restrained her and bore down on her with all his weight in ways that caused her dread. She'd been going on "dates" with him for three months, and with every encounter, he'd gotten a little more aggressive. Just as the tips had gotten a little larger. She was definitely being groomed.

On the first date, the fact that he was more than three times her age and had parched pale skin that felt like ancient papyrus hadn't deterred her. Rich old men came with the territory. She hadn't understood all that came with that package, though, how unpalatable the smell of Old Spice, Bengay, and a hint of urine would be when they combined. How festering his breath from puffing on thousand dollar cigars and the fumes that escaped his stomach from GERD flare-ups. And how viscous his saliva due to his affinity for Jack Daniels and chronic dehydration… the way it stuck to her skin when he raked his mouth across her.

She'd had to completely leave her body to perform for him that night and many nights afterward until she realized that abandoning her body's current sad state for her mind's happy place was at her own peril. He'd gotten more physically challenging, and she had to pay attention to stay safe…

KATRINA HARVEY

 Katrina Harvey is a writer from Chicago, IL with a gift for personal storytelling. With her passion for empowering young women to learn, grow and crown themselves with knowledge, she created the 7 Figure Girls Podcast. She received her B.S. in English from Illinois State University and her MBA in IT Management from Capella University. She and her son reside in Dallas, TX.

AUTHOR'S NOTE: She survived the death of her first love, only to fall in love again and lose herself to manipulation. The truth: all she wanted was love and she had to find it within herself first! She deserved genuine deep love and respect, that unfeigned adoration.

UNFEIGNED ADORATION

I believed…

A little bit about me. I love the rain and rainbows. I believe that as the grown woman I am, I can still be Rainbow Bright, with golden haired ponytails and a small heart-shaped tattoo on my left cheek next to my dimple. All while wearing a rainbow-colored jumpsuit and glitter make-up. I believe in love and all that it brings. The heartache, the pain, the tests of faith, the unnatural bliss of puppy love, and the stabbing regret of why did I stay so long. After it all, I still believe.

Have you ever found old journals, read that crap and said "Damn, I was really wilding out back then?"

Or have you ever read your old writings and thought, "This is 20 years old, but I'm worried about the same stuff?"

Think about it. Have you ever looked at yourself, I mean truly looked at yourself honestly with no filters? Have you ever taken a season, three months, a whole 90 days, no manicures or pedicures, no makeup, and just basked in your natural hair? Have you ever questioned your decisions, your life up to this current point and been like what the hell have I been doing all these years? Have you ever regretted all the things you've done that weren't right in the eyes of God? Have you ever fallen in love with a person that wasn't even capable of loving themselves, yet you expected them to love you?

All I can do is think about how to fix me. Then I have to think, is there really something wrong with me? I've been made to feel as if my choices are wrong. Maybe the timing was wrong, it was off, but it was my choice, right?! It seems all my life I've had to fight myself. An angel on one shoulder and whatever the hell else on the other. Yet even after the duel, nothing. Cause I'm real ... I'm a person that makes mistakes; I just tried to learn from them and not make them again.

It's said "life is only a culmination of daily decisions," and I live by the phrase "live, love, laugh, and learn." Perhaps me being hot in the arse is not helping me at all. But I'm learning a valuable lesson, right?! Yet my sordid tale of love is always haunting me. I feel like I've lost a chance to be in love. Everyone thinks I'm crazy, and I might be, but I can't help what I feel. I'm finally feeling like this is God's move and not mine.

Whenever I seek to get myself together, I do it the same way. I choose to close myself off. No dating. I place boundaries around the toxic people in my life, I block and delete mofos. I try to establish some order and routine in my life. Spend more time with the Lord, and more time with the girls. I work out, go to counseling, meditate, pray, burn sage, do yoga, say affirmations, lose weight, listen to music, get a massage, date myself... With all of this, then, tell me why haven't things gotten better???

"God, sweet baby Jesus, I'm so tired..." she said in surrender.

I remember her so innocent at 19, and he was 21. This was her first serious relationship. They were both in college and they worked together. She had a crush on him for over a year. He seemed so unreachable. He was a supervisor, and she watched as he dated other supervisors. At their job, you weren't allowed to date someone that could report to you, so she just watched him from afar. Until one day, she just had to tell him. She walked in his area to ask a question about electronics, he gave her the answer and back to her work area she went. Except she had to say it.

She picked up the phone and dialed his extension, "Hello, I have to tell you something, I like you!"

He replied, "I know, I been waiting on you to tell me."

Her mouth hung open in shock.

"You were just over here. Why didn't you say it then?" he asked.

"I wanted to but, I don't know."

He stopped her and said, "Give me your number, and I'll call you tonight."

She happily gave him her number, and that night they talked for hours.

They were inseparable from this moment on. He taught her about scary movies and budgeting, and she was happy to learn. For seven months, they loved, laughed, created plans and shared dreams. For seven months, they grew in their relationship, and she knew this was her future, her husband. He was the one.

After her first Sweetest's Day, their first Thanksgiving, their first Christmas, her first New Year's Eve kiss, their first Valentine's Day, their first Easter, it all came down to that seventh month. A week and a half after Easter, eleven days later, on a rainy Thursday evening, he was going to play basketball with the boys, as she was on her way to his house.

"Hey Tiki, where's your uncle?" she said, calling to let him know she was on her way.

"There's been an accident, they don't think uncle is going to make it," Tiki said as she burst into tears.

All she could muster with her voice, all she could whisper was a confused, "What? What!"

Her first love was 21 years old and died of a heart attack while playing basketball. At the age of 19, she was listed in the obituary as his soulmate.

She went away to college, had a child, got a degree, started her career, moved to another state, got another degree and finally stopped living with one foot in the grave. It took 20 years after the death of her first love for her to find love again.

She met her second love online through a dating app. They lived over a hundred miles apart from each other. They began by texting for three weeks before finally talking on the phone. That first phone call lasted until 7 a.m. They just seemed to click.

Finally, after six weeks, they were both out of town in the same city. They met and became utterly attached. They discussed what it meant for them as two single parents to have the kids meet and decided when it happened that would establish a committed relationship between the two. That same weekend, not only did the children meet that weekend. She also met his mother.

He stated, "You've met my mom and my child, we together now."

Her reply was a confused, "NO!"

He came back with "It wasn't a question, it was a statement," as he kissed her and walked away.

She secretly liked a man who could put his foot down.

As she turned back to look at him, she mumbled, "We'll talk about this later."

She required the question to be asked and for it to be answered, so there was no confusion.

After they talked about it that evening, he asked, and she answered, "Yes!"

Her second love was manipulative. He knew what meeting his daughter and mother meant to her, and he lured her in.

Three weeks later, he came to visit her. A month later, they flew to meet her family. All the makings of being integrated into a person's life. Around three months in she became pregnant with twins and simultaneously found out he was talking to five other women. They broke up, she miscarried, became depressed, and got back with him. She just couldn't be in another state, without family, alone.

She felt she needed him. After seven months, she was formally introduced to the church his father pastored. After nine months, the divorce he lied about having was finalized but she continued to find more lies. Her trust in him was tissue paper thin as her depression and disdain for him grew. They had about eight good months together before he proposed, and then things started to crumble again.

Over two and a half years, no matter what happened, no matter who he showed himself to be or the red flags she saw, she gave her fiancé another chance. She believed. She always saw the potential in him, not just his increasingly flawed reality. In his face, she could see the innocence of the little boy he once was, the hurt and pain in his eyes. She wanted to heal him, but eventually had to learn and accept that a man who does not love himself couldn't possibly love her.

The truth: all she wanted was love. She wanted a love of her own.

She grew up listening to fairytales and watching after school specials. Her love of romantic comedies/dramadies ran deep, and she just knew one day that she would meet her knight in shining armor. That he would change her life with a simple kiss. The kind of kiss that would make her tingle and forget her own name. She would know it was him if he held her from behind and kissed her slowly on the neck and shoulder. She had been in love twice, and each one taught her valuable lessons. The first informed her about love and death. The second taught her what happens when the love wears off, but the lies continue, and about living with heartbreak, the need to be resilient, and the perils of lacking self-trust.

No longer dwelling on the past or worrying about the future, she put in the work to be comfortable within herself, for herself, by herself. She sought counseling and asked herself the questions. She talked to God and sat in her loneliness. She lived in her solitude, but was open to critique. She exited toxic friendships, read, and listened to lo-fi music on repeat. She walked, cooked, and purged. She learned, started a business, and became one with I. She, her, and I, is me. Although I've always tried to separate she, her and I, there is no way to separate them from me.

It took the death of my first love, the never-ending journey of raising a young man alone, the friends with benefits, and an ex-fiancé to bring her back to me. I've always looked at each man as if he could be my forever. I've always been a wife without a husband. I still am, but I've learned that grief is a heavy and long burden to carry. I learned that some good dick without good character ain't worth a damn! A good man, don't mean that he's good for you. If I truly looked at the reality of the man and not the potential of him with a dash of me sprinkled in, I wouldn't have been with my ex-fiancé. I wouldn't have had to pick up my broken pieces so much.

I've loved her in pieces but not me as a whole. On Monday, I loved her hair. On Tuesday my brain. Wednesday was a good ass day! Thursday her breasts were popping! Friday my quick wit and charm shined. On Saturday, I allowed her to rest her pieces, and on Sunday, I laid my whole self on the bed, pondering over the pieces. There have been moments when I question every decision she has ever made because, she didn't love herself enough to trust herself. I don't know if that is intuition, God's grace, or simply hindsight. I just know I didn't trust her to make the best decisions when it came to the people she dated, and some of the friendships she made. Even now I work on not trusting her sometimes regarding the things I do day-to-day.

How do I get to the point of loving myself as a whole? Heal to the point of trusting myself and my decisions? How can I empower myself to reach beyond her, beyond the past and be the me I'm destined to be? Do I trust her? Do I really trust me? I have to admit it's all me, every bit of it, was ME!

In my mind, she often yells, "You don't owe me shit!"

She began to realize that she wasn't protecting her, she was hurting herself. She cried, "It's time for me to be me. It means that I have to be selfish. I can't blame her. I have to respect her, accept her, trust me… love me!"

Next time I venture into the world of love, I want it all brand new. I'll just carry a coin purse full of lessons, not a matching set of luggage on this trip. This time, actions speak louder than words; time will be in sync, emotions, thoughts, and ambitions will match. My future will hear of my wounds and know they have been healed. I won't see the pain of his past on his face because he has done the work to be healed within himself, for himself, by himself. There will be a sense of peace and mutual understanding when we merge. He'll appreciate the rain, rainbows, fireworks, love the Lord, but understand I cuss a little. My next love will appreciate the quirkiness of my thoughts, that my laughter is contagious, love giving me foot rubs, and understand my joy for long hot baths while listening to lo-fi, or jazz music, understand what it means to "be my peace" and that I love long and I love hard…

In my dream, I could hear the rain outside my window, as I held the blanket closer to me. The lights flickered through the curtains as the wind howled by. Hearing the rain on the roof, I could feel his arm wrap around my waist tighter to make sure I wasn't asleep. There he was kissing me on the shoulder, I could feel his breath on the back of my neck, as he caressed my arm with his hand. His touch warmed my skin, and I just laid there in his arms and leaned into him as always. He was the peace I needed and in his embrace was my place of comfort. Even with him, I finally understood that, "I am truly the only person I'll have to spend the rest of my life with, and I have to be in love with all of me first!"

I deserve sincere, genuine deep love and respect!

That unfeigned adoration.

DONELL BONAPARTE

Donell, a graduate of Columbia College Chicago (Creative Writing), hails from Chicago, but Mississippi is in his blood, as the Magnolia state was his residence during his teenage years. Southern folks laughed at his Midwestern accent during his time there and Windy City folks laughed at his drawl upon his return. He credits the cancellation of the "Wonder Woman" television show as the impetus to start writing his own tales. When he's not jabbering about writing techniques, storytelling strategies or Patti LaBelle, he works as a mild-mannered sales agent at a great metropolitan hotel. He resides with his husband of 17 years (although the United States has only officially recognized his marriage for the past six.)

"Synthesis" is an excerpt from his soon to be completed novel

Walking to Jupiter.

Author's Note:

"I'm horrible with titles, but I thought of "Synthesis" based on the progression of three ideas: "Thesis," the statement illustrating a point ("Be a man"); "Antithesis," the contradiction of that point (Men don't cry); and Synthesis, the resolution of the conflict between the two.

SYNTHESIS

Zeke Miller's eyes flickered open. A blaring car alarm from the end of his block roused him from his nap. Truman, brown body sprawled across the bed, his head resting in Zeke's lap, still slept soundly. The candle's musky scent lingered in the air, mingling with that of the love the men just made. Stubble prickled at Zeke's fingertips as he caressed Truman's scalp.

WOW.

Zeke couldn't have predicted any of this happening the day he commissioned the mural from Truman. He backed against the headboard and inhaled deeply, letting the satisfaction tingle inside him. The few items of his second-floor bedroom came into focus as his eyes adjusted. The chest of drawers. The easy chair. The wood-framed wall photo of his parents. The king-sized bed. The muscles of the six-foot-one-inch, 210-pound man sharing it with him. When was the last time he experienced this level of closeness with another man? Had he ever?

The Cobalt Cup, the café on the first floor, had always belonged to Zeke's family. So had the apartment. But his recent purchase of the restaurant annex finally fulfilled his father's dream of owning the entire corner building. Wistfully, Zeke smiled in the semi-darkness and allowed his mind to rewind through the years. Hezekiah Miller, Sr.'s one-size-fits-all answer for any situation, echoed through his memories.

Be a man. Be a man.

When Zeke was five, Hezekiah removed the training wheels from Zeke's bike. The boy rode around the block once, then promptly tumbled from it onto the sidewalk. With skinned knees, he scampered up to their apartment above the café. His mother, Odessa, perched the sniffling boy on the toilet seat and applied peroxide with cotton balls. Her sweet humming filled the room as she gently cleaned his scrapes. They were there only a minute before his father came home from work for lunch. He squeezed into the bathroom and stood over mother and son. Without a second thought, he reached over his wife's head and handed a few toilet paper squares to the boy.

"Dry your eyes. Be a man," he said. "You'll live."

"Now, Hezzy! He just fell off his bike."

"Yeah, yeah." Stern, yet caring eyes met Zeke's. "But you won't get the hang of riding it if you stop trying."

So, Zeke wiped his watery eyes.

A few years later, at eight years old, Zeke sat before an open math book on the dining room table.

"I'm so stupid. I'll never get this!"

Odessa, cocoa face weary, hazel eyes sunken, had completed two years of chemo treatments by then. She tightened the scarf around her smooth skull and turned in her chair to face him.

"Don't you EVER let me hear you say that again!"

She closed her eyes for a moment, opened them again, and encouraged him to try the next problem—subtracting fractions with different denominators. Hezekiah trudged through the front door a short time later, having completed the additional errands he'd taken on after his work shift. He took a deep breath and straightened his posture before strolling past the pair and into the kitchen. He returned moments after with a refilled prescription for Odessa and a cold root beer for a frustrated Zeke.

"I know it's hard," he said, squeezing Zeke's shoulder.

Zeke peered up at him. "I don't want to fail the test on Friday, Daddy." He tried to suppress the misery in his voice.

Hezekiah kept his tone steady, refusing to coddle. "You'll lick those problems yet, son. Keep at it. If you fail the test Friday, then you better try *twice* as hard on the next one. Be a man."

His mother nodded her agreement. The dimple in her cheek winked at Zeke when she smiled.

A year later, the cancer finally claimed her.

Six months after the burial, a squawking car alarm awoke nine-year-old Zeke from a spring slumber. His 'Mr. T' alarm clock read 11:43 pm. He got up, went to the bathroom, then to his dad's room to check in on him—a habit he'd developed since the funeral. The bed was empty. Zeke ambled through the house, searching each room, but his father was nowhere within. The boy's stomach fluttered. He might still be downstairs in the coffee shop. But at this hour? Hezekiah always closed up at 8:00 pm sharp and was usually upstairs by 8:30.

The boy padded into the kitchen, entered the pantry, and pulled back a set of shelves, which triggered the electric bulb that illuminated the 18 steps leading down to the first floor. He descended the staircase and reemerged in the hallway at the back of the café. He looked to his left. The shop was closed; the floodlights and overheads were dimmed. Gray shadows washed over chairs, stools, tables, and booths.

The car alarm that woke him up in the first place squawked louder now that he was on the first floor. Then, it abruptly shut itself off, leaving behind instant silence. A twinge of fright rose in the boy. Thoughts of the movie "Nightmare on Elm Street" with Freddie Kruger wielding razor-sharp finger-knives twisted in his stomach. Hezekiah would have told him, "Be a man. You know that stuff in the movies ain't even real." True, but the fact didn't stop his heart from slamming inside his chest. Besides, Zeke had never before been left entirely alone in the building.

Wiping sweat from his forehead, he tiptoed down the hallway toward the swinging doors that led into the kitchen. Porthole windows in the doors loomed over him, higher than his 50-inch frame. Still, he could see that the kitchen lights were on. The boy almost leaped back when he heard the whimper come from the other side of the doors.

Be a man.

He retrieved a Louisville Slugger baseball bat from a corner inside the stairwell, then returned to the swinging doors. He listened closely for a long moment, but heard nothing. He brought the bat up then slowly shouldered the doors open, keeping his body halfway in, halfway out of the kitchen.

Zeke took in the huge rectangular island in the middle of the room. Dozens of scrubbed pots and pans dangled like ornaments from the contraption above it. His eyes swept the area. It was just as his father liked it: "A place for everything and everything in its place." An industrial-sized dishwasher, triple sink, and eight-burner stove lined the right wall. A countertop with small appliances stretched on the left. Dominating the back wall was the walk-in cooler with its chrome door.

A sniffling sound floated from that direction.

Zeke fully entered the room, circling the left side of the workspace. He paused to listen again. Almost a full minute went by in silence before he heard another sniffle. Zeke set his jaw. He gripped the handle and sprang from his hiding space, ready to swing like Hank Aaron.

Hezekiah Miller, Sr. was seated on the stone tile floor, sobbing. His arms hung at his sides; his hands grazed the floor. Zeke was at first confused by the sight of his dad's brokenness, something unfamiliar to him. He had witnessed his father cry just one other time, the day of his mother's funeral. But it was OK to cry on that day; Hezekiah had said so. But this man looked totally defeated. He stared straight ahead at nothing, back slouched against the cooler doors, legs splayed. Zeke's throat tightened as he propped the Slugger against the island and came closer. When he knelt next to his father, he could feel the floor's coolness through his pajamas. He could also smell the alcohol on his breath.

"Daddy?"

Hezekiah moaned softly, but his vacant expression remained.

The boy noticed an open hatbox on the floor in the space between his father's legs. The ceiling lamp gleamed on it, spotlighting a pile of handwritten letters, old pictures, and notes. Most of the pages were still stacked inside the box, but several sheets were strewn on the floor around it. Zeke recognized none of these papers, but he knew that whatever they were, they crushed the only person he called 'hero.'

He spotted a square of paper clutched in his dad's left hand. Curious, he reached across Hezekiah's lap and pulled it free. Hezekiah barely twitched his fingers when the scrap left his grasp. Zeke sat back on his heels and examined what he now recognized as a photograph.

A woman of about sixteen grinned up at him. She wore a white blouse tucked into a long grey skirt. Never had he seen the picture, but the dimple in her cheek was unmistakable.

"Mama."

Her beaming smile was identical to Zeke's. She leaned back against the grill of a large white car, holding a stack of books to her chest. Her mouth was partly open, caught in mid-laugh. Maybe from something the photographer had said, Zeke imagined. Fascinated, he flipped the portrait. The message, written in a tight, curly script, had only partially faded.

"Happy Valentine's Day, Hezzy," Zeke read aloud. "1975. Love, Odessa Winthrop."

The sound of his wife's name brought Hezekiah's mind into the room.

"I love her," he wept. "I swear 'fore God, I love her." His head and torso, still pressed against the cooler door, slid to his right like a clock's sweeping second hand. Zeke scurried and sat fully on the floor, catching his dad as he twisted on his side. He was able to pluck the hatbox out of Hezekiah's path before his feet swept aside the pages littering the floor. Zeke would gather the sheets later. He would ask his father about the box and its contents then. But for now, the boy would hold his dad's head in his lap and simply let him cry. Hezekiah's shoulders shook as he sobbed. "I miss her so much, Son."

Zeke stroked the man's hair and allowed tears of his own to stream down his cheeks.

"I know, Daddy. Don't worry. I'm here for you. I'm here." A rumbling moan from Truman's throat wrangled Zeke back to the now. He cupped the artist's scalp, calmly shushing him. Seconds later, the employee, his Lover, slept soundlessly once again.

Lover? Zeke wasn't sure yet. He would start finding out the answer tomorrow when they went to work—he running the Cobalt Cup, Truman painting the mural in the adjoining restaurant. Whatever discoveries awaited him, Zeke was man enough to handle them.

"I'm here," he told Truman. "I'm here."

KEN COMPTON

A native of the Midwest, Ken discovered the writing bug as an undergrad at Truman State University. He has since become a published writer who has crafted prose across multiple genres that include biblical, family, and relationship themes, and credits Sandra Brown, Harlen Coben, Neil Gaiman, and Walter Mosley as his favorite authors. An active member of the American Writer's & Artist's Institute, Ken is a graduate of the Long Ridge Writer's Group and includes the Saint Louis Writer's Guild among his many affiliations. Writing is God's plan for his life, and he aspires to join the New York Times Bestsellers list. Future writing plans include stage and screenplays.

Graffiti Park is a glimpse into the universe of an upcoming book series.

Author's Note

I dedicate this piece to the loving memory of Mary Rosenblum, my writing instructor and first editor of the story.

Thank you Rainbow Room Publishing for bringing Graffiti Park to print. It was a labor of love and hate with numerous rewrites and near endless editing. I appreciate my growth as a writer since the first draft, and I look forward to the expansion that I am hopeful will induce more love than hate.

Thank you to the readers who will discover how justice is served in a fictional place of mystery and magic where the danger within depends upon what you bring with you.

GRAFFITI PARK

Her body was pinned to the ground under his girth. Her clothes were torn off. She squirmed against the warm soil, the effort more exhausting than helpful, and cringed as he positioned himself between her thighs; he had threatened to slit her throat if she screamed.

What had she learned in self-defense? The practice dummy never attacked, and tucked in the shorts down by her feet, the mace was unreachable. She clenched her teeth to block his slithering tongue but was capable of nothing else.

A beam of sunlight shone through the trees giving her a lasting glimpse of the devil. White. Hair, blond. Beard, scruffy. Eyes, brown and beady.

She laid her head back and rolled her eyes up to darkness; the pleasure in his face was too awful, and the stench of oysters and whiskey was worthy of vomit. She saw someone. An enormous figure had emerged from the shadows against the trees.

He head-butted her and spat, "You stupid bitch."

Her body went numb. She blacked out.

Steve Reichert lay spread-eagled and partially awake under a single bedsheet. He fumbled for his watch on the nightstand.

9:34 AM.

The remnant of bitter scotch intensified his morning breath. Winning Officer of the Year at the previous night's banquet had made it an occasion for more than a Bud Light. Thank God for the rookies who had given him a lift—a few more drinks, and he would have been bound to the bed with regret throbbing throughout his cranium.

The phone rang.

A smack at the speaker button nearly broke the landline, "Reichert here."

"Rise and shine Shit-face," said a baritone voice. "I need you to come in."

"On the first day of my vacation, Chief . . . really?"

"The mayor is on my ass."

"Over what?"

"A rape and assault about three hours ago."

"You're calling *me* in for rape and assault?"

"It happened in Graffiti Park."

Steve sat up and reached for a fresh pack of Newport—the first smoke of the day was his favorite, "I'm listening."

"The victim is a twenty-three-year-old Caucasian female, came in through a side gate in the north sector and got attacked by an unknown."

"What was she doing in Graffiti?"

"An early jogger, new to the city and didn't know about the park's reputation."

Steve took a deep drag and kept listening.

"First responders found a bloody knife on the scene, but no stab wounds on the girl, and no blood trail in sight either . . . the dogs picked up a scent from the weapon but the search came up empty."

"How are we looking with Forensics?"

"The prints on the knife were no good for a match, and seventy-two hours is the latest for a full blood analysis."

"This isn't a lot to start with, Chief."

"You've solved more with less, Sherlumbo."

Steve Reichert's case-solving ability had earned him that nickname. Although he preferred the Lead Detective title, he was less intuitive than Sherlock Holmes but more empirical than Columbo (at least according to his own assessment). "Alright, I'll be there as soon as I can."

"There's one more thing, Steve. The girl saw somebody before blacking out, and we suspect this person contacted Dispatch."

"You suspect? What about the call trace?"

Silence lingered before the Chief spoke again, "There was no call trace."

"Wait, wait, wait—" Steve threw his legs over the bedside, "how was Dispatch contacted?"

"They weren't notified by phone or by anyone in person. Apparently, some strange audio announcement resonated in the dispatch office and said a rape victim would be found behind the north sector's undergrowth. They thought it was a joke but sent a patrol to the area to follow protocol, and sure enough, the girl was there. I don't understand it fully which is another reason why I need you to get this thing done ASAP."

The scar on Steve's lower leg ignited with an itch.

"Steve, you there?"

"I'm here," another moment of silence while he scratched, a thought solidified into relief. "Hey, Chief—" he leaned toward the speakerphone, "what did *this* voice sound like?"

"It was an elderly woman with an Irish accent."

Holy shit, it can't be.

"Okay, I need to see the crime scene for myself."

"Why so sudden, you have a lead on this woman's identity?"

"Not at all, just trusting my instinct," Steve said with guilt in lying.

"Let me have some uniforms meet you at the main entrance. There's a heat advisory today, plus only a fool would go there with no backup."

"They'll only distract me. If you want the best outcome let me do it my way."

The Chief sighed, "Crime-Scene cordoned off the area by the runners' trail. Watch yourself and call in anything you find right away . . . I owe you one for this."

"I'm on it, and you owe me more than one."

The curtains were drawn, but the adjacent hallway light lit the smoky room adequately. Steve looked down the hall at Bane, his Doberman, who was still asleep on the doggy bed. He paced in the bedroom, searching for logic in the impossible and thumping ashes in an empty pickle jar with each pass around the king-sized sleigh.

An elderly woman with an Irish accent, he thought.

She must be three-hundred years old by now.

Steve lifted his leg onto an ottoman. The scar had not bothered him since that night years ago.

Why now?

He bit his lower lip and glanced at the desk where he kept the five-by-seven portrait of himself as a six-year-old standing in front of his parents whose faces he had cutout. Meanwhile, the day's best smoke was burning away. One more deep drag and he dismissed all questions.

Still wet from the shower, his shirt felt plastered around the top of his broad back. He fed Bane and let him out yet skipped his toasted bagel and Sumatra blend, choosing a jumbo pickle and Vitamin Water instead. A quick self-check for keys, wallet, badge, Glock, iPhone, and he was headed to Graffiti Park.

In his new Ford Expedition, waiting at a red light gave him a moment to think about his destination. News networks and reality shows from *Ripley's* to *Unsolved Mysteries* had featured stories about the place.

Years ago, dozens of human skeletons had been discovered there buried from the neck down—the skulls serving as headstones for the gang members who had clashed on the park grounds. The only survivor had been hospitalized with decayed skin hanging upon brittle bone.

"She made the ground swallow us; she made the ground swallow us."

He had never recovered from shock.

A young murder suspect had escaped police custody and been hiding in the park. Days later, an elderly gentleman, dressed in similar clothing, was discovered, claiming to be the culprit. Fingerprints proved that the old man and the murder suspect were the same person.

More recently, hundreds of people had gathered in the east sector for a bonfire, despite a city ordinance outlawing such an event. Rain doused every attempt to create the flame, or so it had seemed. All attendees were stricken with pneumonia, and the death of those who had planned the event was equally strange.

Though skepticism shrouded these accounts, one phenomenon could never be refuted. The Mural Wall, a stone block standing twenty feet high and stretching an eighth of a mile long, stood as Graffiti's central mystery. The portraits, from which it seemed the park earned its name, were ever-changing: Holocaust, 9/11, and the *Hindenburg* disaster displayed previously. The pictures were more thrilling than 3D, but who or what was changing the wall remained unknown.

Its existence dated back to the Civil War as records from 1865 described how Union soldiers used it as intel to defeat the Confederacy.

Some believed the paintings predicted the future. During the 1960s, a mural of a black man lying dead on a balcony appeared. A week later, Dr. Martin Luther King Jr. was murdered while standing on the second floor outside his motel room.

A film crew had once recorded the Mural for a documentary. During the days of filming, nothing out of the ordinary occurred, but all footage mysteriously came up missing.

Nonetheless, the Mural Wall was a part of Graffiti as much as the park was a part of the city. There had been attempts to turn the landmark into a residential area. Still, despite petitions and the support of city officials, all efforts failed for obscure reasons. For the last several years, the entrances had been barricaded with caution tape, and the park remained officially closed.

Steve arrived at the main entrance. A large, rusted wrought iron gate screeched with every inch of opening it. Gargoyle sentries on both sides ushered the way to hell, so it seemed as he drove a spiraling road at twenty-five miles per hour. Easy listening faded to static on the radio. Changing the station and adjusting the volume did not help. On impulse, he pressed the power button on his iPhone, but it was dead, too. His stomach knotted like a mass of maggots squirming in his gut. The better idea of leaving eased the sudden sickness.

But the SUV accelerated to thirty-five, fifty, and seventy miles per hour. The radio blasted Britney and Bach. He grabbed the wheel and slammed the brakes; the Expedition ignored his every maneuver. The doors locked, and the car sped up a hill, forcing him back against the seat while rocks pelted the underside, and smoke from the hood clouded the windshield.

The truck jumped a hilltop and slammed onto the ground.

The seatbelt cut across his waist and shoulder.

The car skidded and sped faster.

He gritted his teeth and scrunched down. His breathing was heavy and sweat stung his eyes.

A small incline, a sharp right turn, a veer to the left, and a sudden dip—his stomach dropped, and his sides ached.

The vehicle turned again, but the speed decreased.

The music faded.

The smoke stopped.

The windshield cleared.

The car coasted to a stop next to a sign that read North Sector.

The engine shut off, and the doors unlocked.

Steve darted out, pulled the Glock, and aimed in all directions.

Okay, he thought wildly, "Okay. OKAY! I'm here. I'm HERE!"

His voice echoed as he remained poised for a reason to fire. The trees, the grass, the air, everything was a threat. He had never killed anyone in his twenty-four-year career as a cop. Would today be the day?

Don't fuck with me.

A quick turn toward the SUV with knees bent and back straight, aiming as if the car was a criminal, he maneuvered around the truck, astonished: no broken lights, no loose mirrors, no worn tire threads, no visible damage. Yet the engine refused to start with the key remote and, after what he had been through, no way would he try the manual ignition from the driver's seat.

The iPhone had fallen onto the floor mat. It was still dead.

A second try with the key remote failed; he would not be allowed to leave even if the car did start, he thought.

Sunbeams roasted his head while pondering the predicament; a Newport would alleviate some stress. Still, the need to keep a free hand and the gun in the other took precedent.

Another scan of the area offered no solutions.

The runners' trail was yards away.

Steve wiped his face with a rough forearm, and, with no other option, started walking.

Except for his Nikes thumping the ground, he heard nothing; no birds chirped; no squirrels scampered; no wind rustled. The trees on either side of the path stood like chess pieces planted strategically for battle.

A robin's nest lay in a tree ahead—a mother and three babies sat inside. The everyday activity of a busy bird tending to open-beaks was absent. Instead, four birds sat almost inert. Their heads turned slowly while he walked by. He paused for something more characteristic. Yet each bird lifted its left-wing as if allowing passage.

On the open acres, seedy grass surrounded a small pond filled with dark, sulfur stinking water. Spider webs engulfed an odious outhouse. Dry rotted picnic tables, shoddy sandboxes, broken swings, and a lopsided jungle-gym had deteriorated the area.

Steve approached a tunnel of forestation where twelve-foot-tall bushes stood alongside trees with low hanging branches blocking most sunlight. Although dark places never scared him, his courage level was lower than usual at the opening of what appeared to be the park's mouth and throat.

The dank cavern emanated a stench upon entering. His nerve diminished once the light from the entrance faded. Specks of sunlight filtered through the crevices to form shapes above him.

A colossal cross nearly coerced him to confess sins and repent.

Steve walked farther.

A giant eyeball glared down at him.

He blinked.

The single eyeball had morphed into dozens.

Before he could run, tree limbs came to life and lashed across the pathway. He shot at the trees, but the branches slithered and bound his legs and arms, paralyzing him like tentacles. A shriek resounded through clenched teeth as the restraints tightened his torso, stretched toward his face and bore into his jawbone and eyelids, forcing his mouth closed and eyes open.

A ball of light materialized from the far end of the tunnel and paneled into a flat screen. Scenes from his past unfolded before him— his mother's infidelities, his father's drug use, and himself as a child hiding under the bed while his parents fought.

The light flickered: the courtroom, the judge, and the custody hearings— the memories flooded back as his anger rose to a fever-pitch. The light flickered again—the molestation from his mother, the beatings from his father. The tunnel went dark, and the vines released their grip. He fell to the ground, limp but soon stumbled to his feet and scrambled to the tunnel's end toward the tape that was just beyond.

Steve staggered to the crime scene and vomited. After the dry heaves, he wiped his mouth and touched his face. No blood, no pain. An oak tree gave support for him to lean against.

Shake it off. It was a long time ago. Fuck them anyway.

His pride would take a hit if anyone saw him like this.

A nervous hand holstered the gun and yanked a pack of Newport from his pocket. The cigarette took the extra effort to light, but the smoke filling his lungs was more welcome than oxygen. He exhaled; the uneasiness settled as the smoke dissipated, yet questions ricocheted like billiard balls at the break.

When did this become about me? And why now? Here?

Appreciation for the Graffiti's silence prompted him to close his eyes and imagine a better start to the day. By the end of the cigarette, he felt more like himself. He dropped the butt and stamped it on the ground.

"Pick it up, Steeben."

Steve drew the Glock, but a crushing blow knocked him down and sent the gun flying. He struggled to regain footing at the sight of who stood before him.

Silver hair rippled from under a black skull cap. Her skin was ghostly white and cracked like chipped paint. Wide green eyes contrasted with a small nose and tiny lips. A long black wool coat swallowed her thin frame, despite the blistering summer heat as enormous hands clutched a tattered purple bag in front.

She was not alone.

Eight white-tailed bucks, with three-foot horns, stood alongside her. An equal number of gray wolves appeared, baring their teeth and growling. Dozens of raccoons and opossums clung to tree barks, while flocks of owls and ospreys swooped onto available branches. Rabbits, moles, and mice scurried in a mass of furry motion.

The park came alive with the uproar of howls and screeches until the old woman lifted a single thick finger. All was silent. She floated to him, "Pick it up, Steeben . . . there be no fire started in this'ere park."

Steve stood, and even at 6'4, he was about two feet shorter than the woman—she hovered just above the ground. He picked up the cigarette butt and shoved it into his pocket.

"My, my, Steeben. Yer has grown into quite a man, tall and broad-shouldered, no longer a runt of a boy."

Steve stared, unable to speak. He cleared his throat and threw his shoulders back, "I need your help."

"Yer searching for that perverted fool of a man, ye are."

"We need to get him off the street before he hurts someone else."

"There be more for ye to figure out here, Steeben."

He squinted, "What do you mean?"

"Yer has forgotten what I taught ye years ago."

Steve maintained eye contact, yet his mind drifted. He felt seven years old again, running through Graffiti the night he learned that his parents would be getting a divorce. In his haste, he had fallen and cut his leg.

Then she had appeared, "Hello, Steeben."

"Who are you?"

"Someone who knows that ye ran away from home."

"I hate that place. All they do is fight and scream."

"Running away is never the answer, Steeben. Somehow, I believe they love ye, even with their troubles."

"What's going to happen to me when they break up?"

"That I cannot answer, only time will tell." She pointed at the cut on his leg, "Let's have a look at dat."

She pointed a large finger at the cut and the bleeding stopped. She covered the wound with her heavy hand, tilted her head, and muttered, "Me yung din, me yung din, me yung din, me, me, me, me yung din, me yung din." Her eyes batted, and her hand glowed green.

He gritted his teeth under the might of her grip until the chanting stopped.

She released him and hovered above, "Go home now, Steeben. Whatever happens, do not hold any anger toward yer mudder and fudder. The hate will poison yer soul and make ye do evil deeds. And evil deeds are always punished."

Young Steve had run. He looked over his shoulder and saw her standing at the hilltop. A second wind propelled him through the park's entrance and across the side street. He turned once more and saw the old woman posted at the gate. He ran without looking back again. Although he could not see her, he knew she was watching him.

The cut had healed by the time he was home, but it had left a scar on his leg.

He had received a merciless beating from both parents.

Steve shook his head, "That was a long time ago, and this isn't about me."

"This is more about ye than ye can imagine. And don't concern yourself over that nasty man."

"That 'nasty man' is still out there."

"Evil deeds are still punished, Steeben." A grin curved her lips, yet there was no humor in her tone.

"You know where he is, don't you?"

She said nothing, but the grin remained.

He lowered his head and said, "All I'm asking is for some clue."

"I've given it to ye."

Steve looked up.

The old woman and the animals had vanished.

Detective Steve Reichert suddenly felt alone, without allies to whom he could appeal for help.

It was just after 1:00 PM when he arrived at the precinct. Some rehearsed bullshit bypassed a long briefing. Steve hated lying to the chief—they had known each other since being rookies on the force but receiving the case file sooner suppressed the guilt.

He studied the artist's rendering on the way to his cubicle, his photogenic memory would be stained with buggy eyes menacing, like a rattler poised to strike. Although rapists rarely changed their appearance, those glaring brown eyes would belie any alteration attempt.

Some details about the victim: Terri Carter, a recent college graduate, had spent all her life in Boise, Idaho. Anger and depression crept in at the thought of horror like this occurring to someone soon after leaving home for the first time.

The psychologist at the victims' unit briefed him on Terri's condition. At the same time, a nurse prepared the young girl for another official visit. After a few moments, he walked in and stopped short. Steve had seen countless victims, yet the viciousness of this attack brought such sadness, he struggled to fight back the tears.

One eye was red, the other was black—exposed splotches of the scalp. Large stitches scarred both cheeks while a massive knot protruded from her forehead. A broken nose had been the butcher's finishing touch.

He introduced himself and expressed his sympathies. An acknowledgment of her bravery in repeating the horrific event served as an empowering tactic. The effort to capture the perpetrator would be as successful as her cooperation allowed.

Terri recounted the attack; his bugged-eyed look, his fish-whiskey breath, his raspy grunts, his painful thrust in and out of her.

Steve visualized the crime scene and placed himself in her position, looking up into the face of the rapist. He envisioned the old woman. What had she done during the assault? What about the blood on the knife? Who had been cut? Was there another victim?

After nearly an hour, he found himself with more questions than answers, but questions pave the way toward leads—the first rule in his work. He gathered as much as he could from Terri's account and promised that the attacker would be caught and punished to the fullest.

The follow-up started by comparing the sketch to images of known sex offenders. It continued with a viewing of nearby store surveillance of patrons buying alcohol and tins of oysters. He leaned on Forensics to expedite the DNA analysis and personally examined the knife—was it new or old, cheap, or expensive? The first day of the investigation was the most important.

To his disappointment, he obtained nothing from his effort. The next step would be to post the sketch on the evening news and wait for potential leads.

By the end of the workday, he had chain-smoked nearly two full packs of Newport. A long night awaited him, he suspected, as Terri's appearance screwed with his emotions. He usually remained detached, but she would be about the same age if he had a daughter.

In the precinct's parking lot, Steve gripped the steering wheel. He glared through the window, replaying the events of the day: the assault, the audio-clairvoyance to Dispatch, the crazy car ride, the shit in the tunnel, the old woman's appearance, and her disappearance. What had she meant about him having more to figure out? Nothing made sense. The possibility of a quickly closed-case faded like a beacon-light in the corner of his mind.

The iPhone beeped with a text:

```
Bud Light Platinum on tap at Thirsty Dogs
B&G . . . come on thru Sherlumbo.
```

A brew and a double cheeseburger with extra pickles teased his appetite, but he dismissed the text.

If this case was unresolved—Steve froze. He reread the text as a question burned into thought—something that he did not ask the chief that morning but needed the answer to now.

A text message avoided a lengthy phone conversation over a question that could lead to everything or to nothing.

The chief's response confirmed a suspicion.

Steve revved the engine as adrenaline surged with renewed hope.

Daylight was burning—no time to tell anyone or do much else.

He had to return to Graffiti Park.

In the west sector, derelict dugouts and bird-shitted bleachers were all that remained of an abandoned baseball field. The record-high heat stung Steve's face upon exiting the vehicle, and, as he trekked the diamond, the seemingly scorching sand infested with red scorpions compounded the uninvite.

Before long, his khakis were stuck to his legs, and polo was soaked at the armpits. He loosened the buttons and pressed on against the humid air. The need for shade accelerated his movement toward the trees in the distance. Still, the faster he walked, the farther away the trees appeared to be. Sunbeams seared him and sweat dripped from his chin. His pace slowed to a plod once he reached the grass. His head spun and vision blurred; mouth hung open, bone-dry. Panting, he trudged a few more feet before collapsing and blacking out.

The sun was gone when Steve awoke. A hacking cough forced him to clutch his chest and jettison the grittiness. Confusion weighed heavily until a replay of the events settled uncertainty with regret. More coughing followed a deep breath; he struggled to rise and squinted at what little was visible.

The moon shone full and blue. High above, the tree branches were like black paint splattered against the illuminated clouds. Darkness shrouded all else.

Returning tomorrow seemed like a better plan, but a vision of Terri flashed and reminded him of his promise to her. Steve clenched his teeth and pulled the Glock.

No turning back.

Along the field's edge, he paced, ready for anything. Trees sheltered the pathway, and the full moon appeared in shards through the branches. Pinpricks of light blinked all about. A twig crackled here and there. Wings flapped overhead. He heard scampering in the brush, and something nearby hissed.

From behind, a heavy thud announced an arrival. Steve turned and met menacing orange eyes surrounded by a shaggy face, short snout, and jagged teeth. The thing lowered its head and growled. He aimed the Glock. Yet anxiety quadrupled when three more sets of orange eyes opened and glowed in the night. Steve stepped back. They moved forward as a bead of sweat trickled his face. He had to stand his ground. Twelve feet decreased to ten with their eyes conveying bloodthirst.

Where is the old woman now?

He swallowed hard. Eight feet. They were twice as big as Bane. Six feet. The savagery stank upon them.

Fuck it.

He fired four shots.

Smoke drifted from the Glock barrel as the wolves lay moaning in agony.

Steve sighed.

If they are meant to live, the old woman can heal them.

The moon appeared at a clearing. The openness eased apprehension, yet Steve remained vigilant, the gun still warm in his hand. Gravel replaced the dirt on the path—a sign that he was getting close to *it*. During the phone call, the chief mentioned that the dogs had picked up a scent at the crime scene, but the search came up empty. Steve had neglected to ask where the search ended.

The air cooled, and the moon brightened, yet all was silent as Steve approached the Mural Wall. Goosebumps prickled on his thighs, and the hair all over his body bristled. Perspiration on his forehead, back, and feet exacerbated the uneasiness as the full length of the wall came into view. The brown mineral was ancient, massive, and imposing. He wondered if it had been expecting him. However, the Mural Wall was blank, an empty canvas. Steve rubbed his forehead, disheartened.

The air became colder with each step toward the center. His face, arms, and hands were frigid. Numb fingertips and visible breath soon followed.

Thunder roared and lightning struck the Mural.

The ground trembled.

He fell back, covered his head and curled into the fetal position as fear intensified.

Lightning struck the wall again.

To his terror, he pictured his tombstone.

Who would care if I died? A few friends. Bane. What would happen to him?

The ground gyrated mercilessly. The wall could topple or the ground could open. Something had to be done, but what?

More questions swirled in what he thought would be his final moments.

Who would capture the rapist? Was the old woman responsible for this?

Steve remembered the gang members who were found buried from the neck down and wondered what his sin was to deserve this.

The chaos lasted a minute that felt like a month.

The thunder ceased.

The lightning ended.

The earthquake stopped.

He lay still, covering his head and gnashing his teeth. The feeling returned to his fingers, yet his hands were sweaty. After a few moments, he stood and checked himself for injuries—thankfully, there were none.

An odor pierced his nostrils—a stink of rotten fish and Jim Beam. He covered his nose and mouth and searched for the source.

What the hell?

A white, chalky outline had emerged on the Mural. The figure held its hands out as if pushing from the opposite side of the rock. Within the odd silhouette, the surface melted and boiled like fillings in a cauldron. Color brightened, and the shape solidified into white skin, blond hair, a scraggly beard, and brown beady eyes.

Something about the image seemed more real than imaginary. He moved closer to touch the face. It felt warm and cold, soft and hard—a mixture of flesh and stone beneath his fingertips.

Moisture streamed from its eyes, and a red substance dripped from its crotch.

"Pleasseeee, help me, help me, have mercy, mercy," said a small voice nearby.

Steve saw no one but an idea in mind.

A business card from his wallet sufficed to dab the fluids—a DNA comparison to the blood on the knife would seal the case, yet no way could he explain any of this.

Too many questions remained. Had the old woman intervened during the assault, disarmed the rapist, and stabbed his crotch before hauling him here? Was the rapist alive, dead, trapped between hell and purgatory, or imprisoned forever within the Mural Wall? Steve was confident, however, that the son-of-a-bitch would never harm anyone again.

The scar tingled. He bent down and rubbed the keloid length of the cut through the pant leg, the old woman's voice about his parents echoed in memory. Do not hold any anger; it will poison your soul and make you do evil deeds.

His father was dying of cancer in a retirement home in the east part of town. His mother showed signs of dementia, residing alone in the house they had all once shared. He had kept tabs on them for selfish reasons but had not seen either one in years. Biting his lower lip and gazing about to avoid the guilt proved useless. His focus fell again upon the wall. The terror on the rapist's face urged Steve to think about his own fate in harboring hatred toward his parents.

Who am I really hurting? Tomorrow, I'll go to visit them.

He was not ready to forgive and forget, but seeing them was a start, at least . . . not for their sake but for his own.

A peace settled in with a sigh, a feeling he had never experienced and did not want to interrupt by overthinking it. Only one concern remained: What justice would there be for Terri with a case that would never be closed officially?

He lit the last Newport and took a much needed drag. The dark surrounding felt less ominous as he blew smoke toward a starless sky. In fact, he wondered about all he had been through during the day, being forced to face old hurts but learning much about his own resilience.

The place of persecution had been the place of salvation, or at least the beginning of it.

Perhaps the same would happen for Terri. The return to the park could be justified as a part of the investigation. It was worth a chance, Steve thought.

An exhale of smoke blown into the portrait's face produced a faint cough from the Mural Wall's prisoner. Steve extinguished the cigarette and placed the butt into his pocket as the tiny voice pleaded more fervently.

He turned to leave Graffiti Park.

A scream rang out.

Steve looked back.

The Mural Wall was blank once more.

CRYSTAL RENÉE

Professor, Editor, Publisher, Entrepreneur, and Author. Crystal Renée is a Christian writer and blogger from the south side of Chicago and founder of *DreamWriterInk!* Writing & Publishing Svs. Her company provides multiple writing services for adults, children, and students of all ages. Crystal Renée uses her 20 plus years work experience in higher education to teach professional and creative writing classes as well as Scholarship essay writing seminars that complement the college admission classes her company offers. It has always been Crystal Renée's personal goal to reduce the learning gap by helping underserved and undereducated students complete their college and graduate degrees. Her expertise has aided hundreds of low-income and students of color complete their degree with minimal to no student debt. Besides owning *DreamWriterInk!* Writing & Publishing Svs., Crystal Renée is currently an English Professor at a Chicago University. In June 2020, she also started a non-for-profit, *DreamWriterInk Youniversity,* for people interested in developing or creating new professional skills that are needed for success in today's job market.

www.authorcrystalrenee.com
dreamwriterink4u@gmail.com
www.dreamwriterink4u.com
(773) 796-3639

AUTHOR'S NOTE: Sisterfriends, what are they? This is the question Carmen, Sadira, and Alexandria attempt to answer after meeting at church on Easter Sunday in 1985. The three childhood friends, now in their late twenties, all led separate lives but push to keep their friendship just as strong as it was when they were younger. But, will the lies, secrets, and deception they foster privately end the divine bond that carried them into adulthood? They were brought together to fulfill a higher purpose. Yet, when long hidden truths are revealed after the sudden death of a close friend, the women question if their bonds of childhood friendships be broken forever. From the upcoming novel of the same name.

IN THE COMPANY OF WOMEN

(Ten years later)

Dee's Story

(Sadira)

Sadira laid there looking at the ceiling of a kitchen that was not hers. She squirmed a little, uncomfortable by the steel-plated faucet that pressed into her fragile spine. Maurice mistook her movements for post-orgasmic spasms and smiled into her neck while pinching the firmness of her bottom that filled his hands. She winced, not at the pinch but because he would not let her go.

"I need to go to the bathroom," she said. Her voice lacked the pleasantness of satisfaction.

"Sorry about that," he referred to the mess he made on the inside of her thighs.

They disentangled, and she walked swiftly to the bathroom, her thighs sticking and unsticking with every step. Sadira had a bad habit of doing this. She was not a smoker or a heavy drinker. There was no satisfaction with coming home and having a drink or smoking a joint to release life's pressures. What she did find herself doing at least once a week was calling a man and going to his house (never hers) and having sex with him minutes after walking in the door. Today it was Maurice because he was one of the few that allowed her to use him. The sex wasn't as fulfilling as he thought but, it was satisfying. It made her feel relaxed and worth something and in control. Those moments provided her something to hold on to, she felt needed and empowered. When she got her fill, when she had touched, grabbed, and bit them enough she felt whole again and the loneliness vanished.

Like most people in her life, Maurice's home had little room for her. The miniature bathroom's once white ceiling had paint curled over that jutted out towards her pointing her to leave. They made the walls appear closer than they truly were. The small octagonal tiles on the floor made her feet cold and the toilet with its seat up was not inviting for any woman. Sadira looked at her reflection in the mirror and through the spots of dried toothpaste and water stains, she saw her empty eyes staring back at her. Her braided hair was partially disheveled and her pink blouse was unbuttoned but, still tucked into her tight skirt.

"Whatever," she whispered to her reflection. This was her routine as well. She often dismissed her appearance after sex. She always looked this way, her clothes never made themselves fully off and no matter how much money she spent on waterproof eyeliner and mascara it always ran, leaving minor dark rings under her short bottom lashes. She appeared like she was crying rather than feeling good. She hated how she looked then and 'whatever' was the magic word that always made the disgust that climbed up her throat vanish like a magician's fluffy white rabbit.

"I left you a clean towel on the tub," Maurice said through the door.
She turned and lifted her short leg on the edge of the tub grabbing the worn towel and wiping herself.

"Damn, you could have given me a good towel."

"Only you, Dee. Only you."

She heard his laugh and was not amused. She was worth a good towel.

'At least once a month I give this man some of my good and he can't give me a nice towel in return. I know he doesn't think it's like that, cuz it's really not,' Sadira thought.

By the time she finished cleaning herself she decided that was the last time she would be seeing Maurice. It was dangerous anyway, she thought to herself. They had stopped using condoms some time ago. That night he claimed he ran out and because of the weather he didn't feel like going to the Walgreens, that was only a few blocks away.

Aunt Maxi always told her never to let a man in without a condom, unless he was special. She told Sadira repeatedly, "Baby girl, once they get it like that, they ain't never gonna wanna go back."

It was true but, Sadira couldn't blame them because sex was so much better without condoms. Every time she stopped by, she reminded herself nothing was that good to catch something or even worse have a kid by him. Maurice was not her man and never would be, they both knew that; it would never work. Sadira was out of his league and besides, she was not interested in commitments nor relationships. At least that's what she told herself every night she went to bed alone.

Now that she was presentable, she looked at herself in the mirror again, fixing her hair and face as best as she could. Finally pleased with her look of composure and control she exited the unwelcoming bathroom. Maurice was in his bedroom that doubled as a living room, he had pulled the bed out of the couch and laid in the middle of it. His feet hung over the edge and his penis was in his hands, working and readying himself for round two.

"You leaving already?" He knew she was not spending the night, she never did.

"Yeah, so get dressed and walk me to my car."

"Damn. Give me a sec."

She stood there uncomfortable, not knowing what to say and having nowhere to sit in his studio. She stood and watched him get dressed. There was little hair on Maurice's body. She liked that about him, he always felt so smooth and clean to her. She delighted in touching him and felt closer to him than the other men she knew. As if the lack of hair made her more in touch with him and her to him.

"You sure you want to leave? You know you don't have to."

"But I do. I would stay longer but I have lots to do tomorrow," she lied.

"Sure. Well, let me give you a goodbye present."

"Reese, I don't want-"

"Who said you had to?" He stood up. "Just sit here," he patted the edge of the thin mattress, "for me."

She did and he kneeled in front of her parting her legs and said goodbye to the only part of her that he ever really knew.

Alex's Story

(Alexandra)

Alexandra pressed her forefinger and thumb into her tight aching eyes. She had lost track of time, but her eyes didn't. They were pink tired from looking at the computer screen without the aid of her glasses. She removed her contacts immediately she entered her house from work followed by her bra. She refused to put on her bifocals because, she didn't know when Tyler, her fiancé, would be home. He hated the way she looked in her glasses so, she chose to look at the online wedding gowns without them.

She sat there in her home office barefoot and looking comfortable in pink satin pajamas. One long caramel-colored leg rested over the other while its foot with Blush painted toes brushed against the newly waxed hardwood floors. She hadn't moved much, afraid the chair would mark up the floor's gleam. The throw rugs would be in on Monday and she hoped Tyler would move this metallic desk and computer equipment before then. She blinked her eyes hard and opened them seconds later to see the sleek cordless phone in her lap. It sat there feeling weightless in the line of her thighs, not because she was really waiting for Tyler to call (but if he did it would ease her anxiety of why he was so late coming home) but, she knew at some point Sadira would call her about some man soon. If it wasn't Dee, she knew Carmen would call and try to explain the Women's Ministry meeting she missed, again. But, the phone did not ring and all the gowns looked identical in color to the white blurs of snow outside. She moved away from the computer, not turning it off, and went into her new kitchen. She made a pot of coffee and sat on the brick island while it brewed. Her house smelled of fresh paint and a strong, 'not-lived-in' odor. Although she and Tyler had been there since August, a month before the engagement it still looked like it was for sale.

The wedding wasn't scheduled until August of the upcoming year which gave her 18 months of planning. Alex wanted an August wedding as a symbol for the day they became a couple. After a year, two months, and a week, Tyler committed to her after her trunk party. However, Tyler was strongly against that date for some reason unbeknownst to her. Together they picked June after her principal duties slowed down. Also, from the economists' forecast, she knew that the economy was going from bad to worse and that depending on Christmas sales there was a strong possibility the New Year would bring either a buyer's market or a huge state budget cut. Parents and the Local School Council were already calling her about fall schedules, supplies, books, new teachers, and coaches for the new fiscal year that begins on July 1st.

It was also a good idea to plan the wedding out now before Debra, Tyler's mother, did it for her. Alex learned from planning her engagement party that Debra held a powerful playing card and was not afraid to use it when it came to getting what she wanted. This annoyed Alex but it also made her respect Debra more because she possessed that same quality. She knew from the moment she accepted Tyler's forced proposal it would be a no holds barred fight with his mother to win. Sometimes, Alex wondered if she was competing for something she thought was already hers.

Tyler loved her, he told her every night. But when it came to his mother, her opinion always seemed to take precedence over his fiancée's. Alex convinced herself this would change once they exchanged vows. All the years she and Tyler had been together she never seemed to notice the strength his mother had on him. It was not until he proposed did she see the sickness of their mother-son relationship. It was admirable for Tyler to be so respectful to his mother. It was of no consequence that his respect poured into all his other relationships with women. Tyler, always a perfect gentleman, treated Alex like the well-groomed lady that she grew to become. She could not say the same for her two childhood friends, who never seemed to fit in her world outside of the church that they met at so many years ago.

Alex poured her coffee into her white ceramic cup and couldn't wait until next June when she would pour her coffee in whatever China set Tyler and she picked out from Neiman Marcus. She let out a squeal of excitement at the thought and heard Tyler come in on the end of her squeak.

He came up behind her encircling her waist, placing his manicured hands on her soft stomach. He kissed her neck and she turned to look at him.

Her man was fine, she thought.

He had peanut butter skin that was accented by his thick chocolate brown hair. His eyes looked into her and he said with total seriousness,

"Call an exterminator, I didn't know we had mice."

"What are you talking about?" Alex said after kissing his lips that were slightly fuller and colder than hers.

Tyler took the cup of coffee she had poured for herself and walked into the breakfast nook. It was colder in there and Alex wished she had put on her slippers. Tyler, just coming in from the cold didn't seem to mind the temperature difference. He sat in one of the wicker chairs and pulled Alex onto his lap.

"I heard a mouse screech when I walked into the house," he put her mug to his lips

"Shut up," she took the cup from him, drinking some for herself.

Enjoying the feel of him under her and the warmth of the coffee mug in her hands and its strength sliding down her throat. Her body smiled at its comfort.

"I got excited thinking about the crystal flutes we'll be drinking out of this time next year."

"It's a shame some glasses can make you make that noise and I can't," Tyler said, removing the half-empty mug from Alex's hand.

"Don't talk like that."

He rolled his eyes and looked up into the glass-paneled ceiling. Alex moved in closer to him, trying to shake off the chill in the room. Snow covered the glass, making the room darker.

"Maybe we should get some kind of defrosters put in the creases so we can see out when it snows."

"That's an idea," Alex repeated Tyler's idea to herself, trying to remember it so she could put it in her planner.

She folded into him and smelled his Cartier cologne and the coffee on his breath that parted her hair with his every exhale. There was another smell there, something florally sweet, but she couldn't recognize it so she let it go and just enjoyed what was right there. Tyler played in her short hair, trying to make it into spikes but it just laid down back in its original place.

"Everything about you is so perfect."

Alex smiled in his chest, half-dreaming. It had been a long day. Life had been long since the engagement and she just wished they could elope, leaving his mother and their families and friends in Chicago. But that wasn't right and what would everyone say on their return? Her mother would be so upset if she couldn't give her daughter the wedding she deserved. She didn't even want to disturb her mind's peace imagining what Tyler's mother would do if they eloped.

Tyler lifted her. Alex woke instantly.

"I can walk."

He looked at her for a second and sat her on her feet.

"I guess you want your feet to get cold."

"I'm fine."

"I know," he flirted, "with your cold feet."

When they reached the top of the staircase Alex turned down the dimmer for the chandelier that lit the foyer and spacious empty living room.

"You don't have to turn that off. I think I might be going back out." Tyler said over his shoulder as he walked into the bathroom.

She followed him and watched him as he watched himself in the well-lit mirror. He looked at his face, running his soft hands over the smoothness of his cheeks and chin searching for an answer to the question to shave or not.

Alex stood in the doorframe watching him unbutton his tailor-cut shirt. Revealing his sleeveless Ralph Lauren undershirt. The muscles of his chest made him look like a model for the designer.

"You just got home and the weather's bad."

"I know but its Friday and I promised the fellas."

"Where are you going?"

"To some sports bar in the city," Tyler was always vague and he knew Alex hated when he was.

"I thought we were going to discuss the party."

"I thought you and Mom handled all that."

"I am not engaged to your mother, Tyler."

"I know but she likes to do that kind of stuff. Just humor her, Alex."

He walked to the toilet and lifted the seat. Alex rolled her eyes in disgust and closed the bathroom door as she heard Tyler's pants unzip. She went into their bedroom and tried to figure out the most efficient and effective way to steer this conversation. She didn't want to argue but she did want to know what was going on.

Tyler came into the room barefoot with his shoes in one hand and his shirt in the other. He hummed the new Mary J. Blige song while walking to his closet.

"You know for all that crap Mary went through she sure looks good. Black women know they age well."

"Tyler."

"Baby, I'm being serious. Look at Tina Turner. Ike Turner put her through hell, may he rest in peace, and she doesn't look older than 55, if that."

He knew she was upset and instead of approaching the subject, Tyler chose to ignore it. It wasn't making his situation any better. He stood there in his closet talking to his wardrobe. He walked into it and with her anger and the lowness of his voice she could barely make out what he was saying. She heard the names Diahann Carroll and Cecily Tyson as he continued his one-sided conversation.

He came out of the closet with a cream sweater and a pair of brown wool slacks. He laid them on the California king with Alex. She looked at him in disbelief. She couldn't' believe he was completely ignoring her. She knew he knew he was wrong because he continued to talk, and he did not look her in the eye once. He went back in the closet and after a minute he emerged with a pair of brown Kenneth Cole loafers.

"Tyler."

"Yes, hon."

"I don't want you to go out tonight. I would like for us to spend some time together."

He looked at her, not wanting to say no, but he definitely wanted to go out. Alex read the struggle in his eyes but as usual, she refused to give in to his silent request. The weekends were the only time they got to spend together and she wanted to be with him tonight because it was too much stuff going through her mind to deal with alone. Tyler refused to comfort her as she needed.

"I already told the fellas I would meet them. I'm already running late. I should have just met up with them without coming home." He said with nonchalance.

His words stung Alex but his tone made the pain stay twice as long. So many times when they had these little quarrels he would say things with the most arrogant nonchalance. After all these years she still didn't know if he was totally unaware of the pain he caused or if he was just a jerk that used nonchalance as a cover like Sadira keeps saying. They barely argued and because Alex was a woman that liked to avoid drama and arguments she never questioned him. However, tonight she wanted to because she was beyond irritation from her day and she wanted him to stay home because she asked. Alex knew if she made a fuss Tyler would think it as a ploy to keep him home. The argument would only escalate, and Tyler would leave and spend the night at his mother's.

"Tyler I am only going to ask you one more time. I want you to stay home with me tonight."

"I really want to, believe me, hon, I do. Who wants to drive on those slick roads? But the fellas are already waiting for me at The Spot. They give me a hard enough time because I'm always with you anyway. I promise I will be back by midnight."

She was silent. She knew he would be back after midnight reeking of liquor and cigar smoke. He might make it home by two if he got bored.

She watched him dress. He took his time, as usual, making sure every crease was right and every pleat laid flat. He made several trips to their master bathroom each time coming out with a new scent. First, it was the scent of Crest Whitening toothpaste, then it was his cologne, and finally, it was the Listerine mouthwash. Usually watching him dress made her proud and a little excited, she knew the impression he made on those around him. It was different tonight because with every confident action he took, Alex felt her anger build and she swallowed it down, remaining composed as she always did.

She pretended to read the December issue of Black Enterprise, but the words could dance around the page for all she noticed. Her gaze drifted off remembering when she was twenty-three and he was twenty-seven and, all she had to do was look upset and he was there at her side giving her what she wanted when she wanted it.

It hadn't always been that easy, Alex remembered as she heard the front door close. She couldn't pinpoint the day she lost control over their relationship, but she did remember when she fell in love with him. She remembered that he left the New York office just to continue their relationship. Alex didn't make empty threats and Tyler new after 8 years of playing games with Alex she meant what she said. If he hadn't come back home she wouldn't be worrying about him and his 'fellas' on a Chicago snowy night. Her left ring finger would be lighter and not as brilliant without the 3.5-carat platinum Tiffany ring that now adorned it either.

Alex knew once he moved back to Chicago, Tyler would truly love her as much as she loved him. She was sick of doubting his love because he betrayed her so many times while they were long-distance dating during her college years and with his internship turned job in New York. She knew his returning home would lead to her engagement and then the dispelling and other women, including his mother. Tyler was always honest with her about these things, well as honest as she thought, and that is why she stayed with him for so long. She trusted him and respected him for his honesty, something Tyler defined as loyalty, but Alex saw different and that is why she gave him the ultimatum before she allowed herself to fall deeply in love with this man who had always known her so well.

She laid in her bed thinking all this and tried not to get any more upset. Tyler was her equal in so many ways. She couldn't construct a better mate. There was always something about him that drew her to him no matter what he did and, Alex thought that must mean something. Despite his past affairs and his loyalty to his mother, he was hers and Alex put her glasses on turned her tablet, and picked up her phone.

"Hey Dee, you busy?"

Carmen's Story

"Where are you? Why aren't you answering your phone? Anyway, your girl is getting on my last nerve. Call me back." Carmen erased the message Sadira left on her phone.

Carmen smiled as she placed her Bible in the passenger seat, the back seat was occupied with Lil' Mike's books and Janelle's car seat. She had just come from Bible study and was trying not to hear Sadira and Alex's drama. Today's Biblical lesson was on patience. The group's goal for the week was to be more like Job. Whenever her patience was running thin, she was to think of Job. She drove home in silence and was enjoying the silence and solitude of her car before the volume would be raised when she walked in her home.

The streets of Chicago were full of black and gray dirty snow that matched the CTA buses. She paused a little longer at a stop sign and let a few people fighting the wind cross in front of her 2008 Ford Escort. When she let the hesitant mother and son walk too, the car behind her blared its horn. She ignored it because she knew how that woman felt, who dragged the little boy across the street. She knew the weight of those bags she carried and the urgency the woman felt to get her child out of this weather.

She said a silent prayer for her patience and the car behind her, then pulled off. In her mind she planned out the dinner she would have to cook as soon as she walked in the door. The greens from Sunday, boxed mash potatoes, and baked chicken sounded like a good plan. She knew Mike and the kids would rather have the chicken fried. It would be quicker, but she didn't feel like standing over that stove, nor did she want to deal with the guilt she would feel once she swallowed down two double battered and dipped chicken thighs in hot grease. She called herself dieting but eating that king-sized Snickers for lunch did not help. She had to lose fifty pounds by Alex's wedding. She called her house and hoped Mike had cleaned or at least started dinner as she asked him to that morning before he left for work.

"Hey babe," Mike said answering the phone.

"Hey, I'll be home in five minutes, could you come out and move the chairs from our spot in front of the house?"

Mike spent an hour shoveling the 3 feet of snow that had fallen the night before. When had he finished he placed two of their folding chairs in the spot he dug so none of their neighbors could enjoy the fruits of his labor.

"Who is going to watch your daughter while I stand outside?"

"Let Lil Mike watch her."

"Yeah right."

She did remember what happened the last time they left 8-year-old Michael Jr. in charge of his two-year-old sister. Carmen entered the house and Lil Mike had Janelle in a headlock and was pressing his knuckles into her soft naps. Janelle was screaming so loud and choking on her tears and spit, Carmen was afraid someone would call DCFS on her.

"Ok. Well, I will be home soon."

She didn't even bother to ask him if he had taken the chicken out the fridge when he got home from work. She knew as soon as he hung up the phone he ran to the kitchenette and started running cold water over it.

She was right; after placing her bags and wet boots on the living room floor next to her husband and children's wet boots, she caught her husband standing over the sink rinsing the chicken. He had neatly piled the dirty dishes on the countertop next to the line of Kool-Aid ringed glasses.

"I'm sorry, honey. I forgot."

"You forgot to wash the dishes too?"

"I was tired when I got home."

"And I'm not?"

He was silent. He looked down at the chicken that was turning from pink to white.

"Is that water hot?"

"Yes. I'm trying to defrost it."

"No, you are cooking it." Her voice rose, "Just move Michael. Please move," she said calmer. In the back of her mind, she wished he would move. Move the chairs out of the parking spot. Move his body and do something besides go to work and sleep. Move out of her house.

"I didn't mean that," Carmen said to the chicken she was cleaning. "Where are the kids?"

"Lil Mike is playing some video game and Janelle is sleeping."

"Michael you know she will be up all night now. And has your son finished his homework?"

"He said he did."

"Did you check it?"

"You are better at that than I am."

"He is in second grade. You mean to tell me you couldn't even check his homework." She finally yelled. She forgot she just left church. Job was far from her mind. She forgot the Holy Ghost was working within her. She turned around and opened the oven door.

"You're not frying the chicken?"

"No."

"Why not? You know you have the best fried chicken. It's even better than my momma's."

His charm was not working today. She just looked at him and was glad a clean knife was not in her reach.

"Because my feet hurt, and I am not going to stand over a hot ass stove. I know you aren't going to do it either because you can't even defrost the damn chicken let alone cook it."

"You want to have an argument?" Michael challenged. "Why don't you smile for a damn change?" He stormed off.

She did fry the chicken. She didn't care if the grease would stick to her already large hips and thighs. Once the argument ended and the chicken sparkled a golden hue, Carmen gave her husband the smile he wanted. She delighted in the crunch and the spiciness of her chicken.

Her family of four sat at the card table that was placed in the living room that doubled as a dining room during meals. The crumbs from their meal mingled with crumbs from previous meals eaten there throughout the week. Lil Mike went on and on about his day and how he wanted to go to somebody's birthday sleepover. His parents paid him little attention, but his baby sister hung on to his every word. Often repeating his speech, not to mock him, but because she admired her big brother.

"Mama, make her shut up," her son whined.

"hut...up," Janelle repeated, emphasizing the t on shut and p on up.

"Don't say that," Carmen told her son over the smacking of Mike stuffing his mouth.

"Why not?"

"Because I said so. Boy, don't you ever question me!"

Lil Mike looked at his daddy, who grabbed another piece of chicken. Mike was good at ignoring his kids when they annoyed him.

"May I be excused?"

"Scuse-duh," Janelle said, turnip green juice spraying out her mouth.

"Yes, but read a book, do not turn on that Play Station."

"But I did my homework. I don't have nothing to read."

"Well read your Bible."

"Ma," Lil Mike whined.

"Did you say something?"

"No ma'am."

"Ma'am?" Her daughter wondered who ma'am was. Janelle looked at her brother and pointed at Carmen and said, "Mommy."

Carmen felt like Mommy all the time. Was she really a ma'am? Was she ever anything but Mommy? It seemed everything she did was for her kids. She even started going to Bible Study to improve her mindset and spirit when dealing with her three kids, Lil Mike, Janelle, and Big Mike. She looked at her husband of nine years and wondered what the hell she had gotten herself into. She did love him but wondered how much he still loved her. He didn't love her enough to help around this house. He saw her struggle to keep their house and life in order but did nothing but sit in the living room and watch TV.

He took care of them and was a good father. But often time she wondered, shouldn't there be more to a marriage? Something more than her being Mommy and him being Daddy? Michael felt his wife's gaze and tried not to acknowledge her. That pissed her off too. He knew something was bothering her. How can you be in a relationship with someone for almost twelve years and not care to know what was wrong?

"The chicken is good." He told his plate instead of his wife, refusing to make eye contact.

"Thanks, I guess."

Carmen finished her third piece of chicken and went into the bedroom and slammed the door. She heard Janelle yelling for her then the voice of Mike pacifying his little girl.

Carmen got on her knees and prayed to Jesus to help her.

Dear Lord, I come to You giving you total praise and thanks for my family. Pastor said that even in our worst moments to praise You. Bless Your name. I praise and magnify You. Jesus, I ask You to help me become a better wife and mother. Please God, please show me how to make things better.

In Jesus' name, I pray,

Amen.

Later that night, after she checked Lil Mike's homework, cleaned, and put the kids to bed. From their bedroom, Carmen heard Michael in the kitchen running dishwater. The water stopped and she heard his steps coming towards her. She was in their full-sized bed, reading admission information to Chicago State University.

"Did you find anything that interests you?" Mike said waving the white flag.

"I have found too much that interests me."

"Well, I know something that has always interested you."

He moved to the bed kissing her would be knee that peeked out of the oversized night tee.

"Do you really?"

"Ummm hmmm. And I know what has always interested me."

His hands slipped under her shirt to slide over the double rolls of flesh that lined her should be a waist. Mike's hands sought her heavy breast that spilled into the pits of her underarms. As his rough hands glided over her, Carmen began to feel sick, disgusted by what he must be thinking. As usual, she imagined Mike holding in his disgust at her fat. How could he be attracted to her blob of a body? A woman who couldn't even fit the wedding ring her husband bought.

"I thought you were washing the dishes."

"I rather wash something else. The dishes aren't so sexy when they are wet."

This talk meant nothing to her anymore. She knew Mike was just trying to make her feel better. She knew she didn't excite him. The dishes were probably more exciting.

"Mike, how about you finish the dishes and I will wait here for you.'

"You promise?"

"Yeah," she thought she sounded convincing. When he left out the room she moved the books off the bed and slid under the covers. She closed her eyes and prayed she would be asleep by the time her husband was done in the kitchen.

(The Beginning)

"Your momma ain't buy you nothing new for Easter?" Sadira asked the plump girl whose dress had been white two or three Easters ago.

"Shut up, Dee," Alex said. The white patent leather of her shoes squeaked as she crossed her ankles.

Sadira stared at Carmen, the quiet new-comer. When Carmen realized the smaller girl was determined not to break first, Carmen gave her a closed-mouth grin.

"Where you from, Carmen?"

"I stay on Jeffery." Carmen gave a full smile this time, the white of her teeth contrasting with the darkness of her skin. It excited her that this girl, Dee, remembered her name from when Mrs. Murphy introduced the girl to the Sunday School class.

"Where?"

"Dee," Alex interrupted, looking at Sadira through the thickness of her heavy bangs that fought with the length of her eyelashes.

"It's ok," Carmen sat down next to Alex, trying to cross her bare legs just like Alex. Her patent leather squeaked too, but unlike Alex, the friction of Carmen's cheaper shoes caused a black mark that matched other ones from previous years.

"I live on 72nd and Jeffery."

"My Auntie stays over there. She live with her boyfriend Ray. You know them? My aunt look just like me. And her boyfriend Ray is fine. He light-skinned-ed, with curly hair. My daddy say he must be Puerto Rican, cuz his family stay in South Chicago. You know them? Maxine and Ray?"

"No, but my mommy might. She stays outside a lot."

"You don't go outside with her?" Alex asked before Sadira.

She knew her friend would ask Carmen question after question until the adult service started. If that happened Alex wouldn't be able to sneak a sip of the Orange Crush Sadira always bought her between services.

"Naw, I stay in the house and watch my little brothers and sister."

"How many you got?" Sadira cut her off.

"Three brothers and a little baby sister. She turns three on Friday."

"Damn, you got brothers and a sister? I ain't got none."

"Girl, don't curse in here," Carmen said.

This was her first time in a church since her grandmother died two years ago. She used to get so excited when her grandmother picked her up on Sundays and brought her to the church. Carmen felt it necessary to tell Sadira not to act like her mother in the house of the Lord.

"Sorry, I forgot." The tiny girl blushed.

"How old are ya'll?"

"We are both 10. Alex is older than by 6 months and two days. How old are you?"

"Eleven. I turned 11 on Valentine's Day."

"That means boys will always like you," Alex said as if she really knew.

"Girl, who said that?" asked Sadira.

"Just think about it, Dee." Alex adjusted the elastic string of her Easter hat.

"I got a boyfriend."

"Really?" Sadira and Alex said in unison.

"Yeah and he's in the fifth grade. His name is RanDell Wilcott, and he is fine"

Instantly, Carmen gained a new respect from the two. Sadira and Alex asked her question after question. Carmen answered them all, unhesitating. Some questions she didn't think she should answer in church. She felt like God was watching her today because the teacher had said that today was the day Jesus rose from the dead and she knew He was there just waiting for her to do something wrong. It was her first day back and she didn't want to upset Jesus. Instead, she told the girls she would tell them after church.

Carmen wasn't the only new girl that came into the Sunday school class, but to Sadira, she was the most interesting because she had a bra on and her dress wasn't new like everyone else's and her shoes were dirty and her hair was not combed. Her short hair struggled to stay in a black rubber band at the back of her head. Her edges were so nappy, Sadira instantly knew that Carmen hadn't spent any time in her parents' kitchen getting her hair pressed for church. The girl's dinginess showed her to be different and this is what piqued Sadira's interest. Sadira didn't own a bra because she had nothing to put in there and she got a new Easter dress, matching purse, and identical shoes, every year. It was hard for her to comprehend why Carmen did not have any new clothes for Easter Sunday. Alex also noticed Carmen's difference but like most nine-year-old kids the wonder of why Carmen was different did not stay with her past Carmen's initial introduction by the teacher. New kids came to church every Sunday, especially on Easter but only half of those had parents that were members. Carmen's appearance in class would have gone unnoticed had it not been for her friend and neighbor, Sadira.

Easter Sunday always brought a large number of folks to church. Pastor McKinley anticipated this Sunday, knowing the holiday would bring three times as many people to the freshly built church. In 1981 New Zion Non-Denominational was welcomed by the neighbors of the South Shore community. Like most Black churches, New Zion started as a storefront, lodged between a laundromat and a beauty shop on 79th and Exchange. The small church had a loyal congregation of twelve that grew to a little over a hundred in five years. In those five years, the church's building fund worked endlessly, securing donations and neighborhood support for a new church. The work paid off and this Easter was the fourteenth day of the newly built church.

New Zion became a mosaic of spring pastels; vibrant fuchsias, lush purples, grass greens, and butter yellows warmed the cool Chicago weather. Adult Sunday school was over, and the adults left the sanctuary to find their children, talk a little, or grab a drink before 11:00 am service. The girls' parents found them sitting together in the classroom, comfortable like old-time girlfriends, one in a too-tight dress and no tights, the second with long legs ahead of their time, whose white-gloved hands kept finding their way into her sandy brown hair, the third much smaller than the others in perfectly matched eggshell blues from head to toe and large sad eyes. Rhonda and Natalie knew their two daughters would be together, but neither of them recognized the third girl.

"Mamma," Sadira got up, and ran into her mother's waist, trying to wrap her arms around the prettiness.

"Child stop. You're going to wrinkle my dress and mess up your hair." Rhonda detangled her daughter from her.

"Hi Ms. Sadira, don't you look lovely today?" Natalie said, embarrassed that she hadn't thought to buy matching outfits for her family. But she knew Alex was classier because of her hat and gloves.

"Thank you, Mrs. Dickson."

"Alex, that hat you have is sharp, girl. Where did you get it?"

The mothers began to talk over their children. Carmen stayed in her seat, praying silently to Jesus that her mother wouldn't come in and embarrass her. Her mother a non-churchgoer, heavy smoker, and drinker, had decided to wear dated flared pants and the one loose shirt she owned to the church. Her baby sister was the only one who had a new outfit, but even that was a four-dollar dress they had picked up a few months ago at Zayre.

"Hey girl," Sadira said to Carmen, "where's your momma?"

"Sadira, stop talking so loud," said Rhonda Young.

Carmen got up and moved away from the pretty girls with nice and pretty mothers who smelled clean and soft like petals. "I don't know where she is. I probably should go find my brothers anyway."

"Mommy, where's Brad and Jonathan?" Alex asked, once her mother and Mrs. Young finished speaking.

"With your father. We should probably go up to the sanctuary, it's almost eleven," Rhonda Young looked at her watch, kept on her left arm not because she was right-handed but because it allowed her to show off her diamond wedding ring and eternity band.

"Come on, Sadira, tell your friends goodbye, I am sure your daddy is wondering where we are."

Sadira rolled her eyes at Alex and Carmen. She knew her daddy wasn't looking for them. He knew where they were. Sadira thought about saying that aloud but decided against that. She didn't want to get spanked on Easter, especially in front of her friends.

"Carmen, don't forget after church," she whispered.

Carmen nodded and followed Sadira and her mother out of the classroom. She hoped the two girls would not forget about her after church. None of the girls at her grammar school really liked her, they thought she was stuck up because she chose to stay inside during recess and read her Sweet Valley Twins books. Carmen loved to read and school was the only place where she had the silence to read without being bothered. When she got home she would have to take care of her mother and her siblings. She wondered what her mother was doing. She hoped she would stay for the entire service. Carmen saw her mother through the windowpanes standing in front of the church her sister in one arm a cigarette in the other hand. Her little brothers played around her yelling and screaming. Carmen felt embarrassed by the looks the members of New Zion gave her mother as they entered the church. Carmen decided not to go outside but walk into the sanctuary. She had no clue if her mother was going to come inside but she knew how to get home and was not afraid to walk the mile back to her house alone.

In the church, she thought of her grandmother and how proud she would be of Carmen. How she forced her mother to take her brothers and sister to church on Easter Sunday. She knew Grandma would want it that way. Carmen then began to pray that the two girls she just met would be her friends forever.

*****

(Seven years later)

They each sat on sides of the undersized cafeteria table eating greasy shoestring French fries and drinking RC Cola. The sound of their adolescent giggles and high pitched voices harmonized with the music of other teenage conversations that frequently filled the classrooms and halls of Miller Magnet high school.

Sadira, Alexandra, and Carmen attended one of Chicago's better public high schools. Out of a class of about five hundred students, they were not the most popular but, they were not the nerds either. They fell somewhere in the middle of the "oh-so-important" popularity ranking. They were comfortable in their place because they had the luxury of enjoying both ends of the spectrum. Unlike the popular kids, the three didn't feel the pressure to wear designer names each and every day. But, they were high enough on the list to own the required Coach Skinny Case and the whiter than white pair of K-Swiss gym shoes.

"Dee, there's Maurice." Alex nodded in the direction of Sadira's crush.

Reese Turner walked into the cafeteria. His head bobbed to the beat of the rap that blared through his earmuff-like headphones. Sadira felt her heart begin to beat to the same tempo. She tried to hide her smile by stuffing three fries in her mouth.

"Girl, just let it out," Carmen said to her.

"Shut up" Sadira smiled.

Her gaze followed him to the cafeteria line. Maurice stood there not paying attention to anyone. Instead, his hazel eyes stared blindly into space. His Girbaud jeans hanging around his thighs and the blue and red-stripped Polo shirt covered all the parts Sadira wished to see. As the line moved, Maurice kept pulling his pants up in sync with the beat in his ears.

"Don't do that," Sadira said to Maurice but only her friends could hear.

"Dee!!" Alex blushed.

"What? I'm just being honest. All that height and those big feet gotta be a sign for the real deal."

"Just go talk to him," Carmen urged Sadira.

"For what? So he can laugh in my ugly face and tell me to take my scrawny ass home?"

"How do you know he will say that?" asked Alex.

Sadira didn't respond. She just rolled eyes fixing her gaze on Maurice's lips.

"Damn I wonder what those lips would feel like on mine, upper and lower."

"You are the horniest little person I know," Carmen said.

"Well, I don't get mine on a daily like you. And don't talk to me like I'm a midget."

"Do we have to talk like this?" Alex was so sick of talking about sex. Every lunch period it was the same thing.

"Ever since you moved to the suburbs, you been trippin'," Sadira said to Alex.

"Dee," Carmen pleaded.

"What? Don't act like you don't think the same. We been friends too long not to admit when one of us is trippin'," Sadira shot Carmen a look.

It was true. Just the night before, Carmen and Sadira talked for an hour or so about how Alex was acting funny with them. They were just getting to the heart of the problem when Carmen's mother made her get off the phone. That's why Carmen didn't respond. She just wished Sadira hadn't put it out there like that. It caught both Alex and Carmen off guard.

Sadira looked at them, not understanding her best friends' surprise. They knew how she was. They knew she couldn't bite her tongue and if she could she just wouldn't. Sadira didn't even understand why she had to. They had been friends for ten years, they were practically sisters. Sadira just couldn't understand why she had to watch what she said. She knew sisters looked out for each other and would do anything to preserve their friendship. Not that Sadira had any sisters of her own to prove her theory but that's what all the TV shows taught her.

"I think what Carmen is trying to say is that you should be more tactful in your statements," Alex explained, choosing to ignore Sadira's comment.

"See that's what I'm talking about. What the hell are you talking about? What teenager that you know talks like that?"

"A lot. Just because you don't doesn't mean that I am trippin. I don't know what the hell you're talking about. I haven't changed. Matured maybe, but that has nothing to do with me moving to the suburbs."

"Yeah, ok whateva," Sadira rolled her eyes.

"Alex, I think what Dee is tryin' to say is that things are different, the only time we really get to hang is at school. I mean what woulda happened if we all had different lunch periods?"

"We would still be girls. Nothing has changed." Alex began to feel uncomfortable. She looked at the other two; Carmen sat there, her brown eyes searching to understand Alex's side. Sadira looked away from the two with defiance.

She knew things were falling apart. They all did, Dee was the only one willing to verbally acknowledge it. She missed when it was always just the three of them. Sadira loved Carmen just as much as she loved Alex but it just didn't feel right not having Alex there to accompany them on their walks through the neighborhood and their car rides to and from school in Alex's car.

"For real, nothing has changed," Alex confirmed to them and herself.

"Yeah, whateva," Sadira responded.

To prove her point Alex drove them home. This was the first time in months that she had been back to the neighborhood where she spent her first seventeen years. To her surprise, it was still the same, not that it should be any different from those that lived on the block. They drove down Marshall Avenue and, she remembered all the identical brick houses. The two-level houses, some with finished basements most without. All of them had porches that connected to five concrete stairs that spilled out to sidewalks that now looked narrow to Alex. The lawns appeared much smaller also and the houses seemed closer than they should be. Maybe suburbia had changed her, Alex thought as she drove. She felt like an outsider in what she had known as home.

She regretted offering to take her friends home, she was afraid of what else she would feel and what else would look different. Sadira sat in the passenger's seat singing the words to the third R. Kelly song playing on the radio. Carmen sat behind them reading. As they pulled up to Sadira's house Alex took a deep breath, trying to push down the wave of anxiety that was trying to drown her. She pulled up to the house searching for a reason not to stay.

"Good there's a space right in front." Sadira pointed her slender index finger that just made it past the dashboard.

"Damn girl, that book got too many pages," Sadira said, putting her book bag over her shoulders.

"Yeah, and it's boring as hell. The Grapes of Wrath is not nearly as good as Beloved."

"What do you expect when you take an A.P. class?"

"The books aren't boring to me. You should've taken it with us." Alex clicked on her car alarm.

"Yeah, whateva, I wanted to enjoy my senior year of high school. And ain't nobody tryin to take your car, Alex."

The smell of Glade plug-ins engulfed them as they walked into Sadira's house. The house was quiet and as always looked freshly cleaned. The three took off their shoes at the door and put their bookbags in the front closet. The closet door whispered across the thick carpet, that was the color of wet sand. The abundantly plush carpet made the furniture appear to float on the carpet that always looked brand new. Ten or more plants decorated the living room, practically covering the large bay window. Their slick green was the only color in the room. The rich brown leather couch set complimented the carpet perfectly. The couch and love seat looked too comfortable to sit on, which was good because the three knew they never could. Seven pictures lined the never used fireplace, six of them were of Sadira's parents starting with their prom picture on the far right and ending on the left with a picture from their second wedding. Evenly dividing the six was a picture of Sadira. It was the only one that ever changed; a new picture of her was replaced yearly as she advanced from grade to grade. However, all the pictures looked new because not one particle of dust ever lay on any of the picture frames.

"I'm home," Sadira yelled. No one responded. Sloppily, she dropped the mail on one of the two faux cedar tables.

"Who you thought was gonna be here? It's not even four." Carmen said.

"You tryin' to be a smartass, huh? Auntie Max was supposed to be using the computer to work on her resume."

They went upstairs to her room, where Sadira changed her clothes.

"When was the last time your mom came up in here?" Carmen asked.

"She doesn't."

Sadira's room looked like two snakes had been fighting in there with a cat or two. She had clothes all over the place. Magazines decorated the mess giving it just the right teenage appeal.

"You should never invite anyone up here," Alex said making a space for her among the stuffed animals and she hoped clean underwear.

"Who would be up here? It's not like I got a man or anything."

"Girl, they don't care," Carmen spoke from experience, "all they care is that you're clean."

"Let's go," Sadira said.

"Wait I wanted to look through your tapes. I haven't had a chance to buy any new music," Carmen said as she rose from her space on the floor.

"Yeah, me too."

"I'll tell you what I got later. I want to get out this house before my mom gets home."

"What's the rush?"

"I'm on punishment."

"For not cleaning your room?" Alex didn't have to guess, Sadira was always on punishment for not doing something her mother told her to do.

"Yeah. What's the point in always cleaning when it's never clean enough for her?"

The 'her' referred to was Sadira's mother, Rhonda. Rhonda Young was from the old school. She believed the upkeep of her house reflected her. Every day she came home from work and cleaned something. She would make dinner for her family and when Sadira didn't clean the dishes right after dinner, she did it herself. Once the house was clean enough, she would spend the rest of the evening with her husband, who would watch television until he fell asleep. Sadira didn't understand the life, if you could call it that, her parents led. Once she had caught her mother staring at her father while he slept in his TV chair. Sadira immediately became embarrassed, feeling like she intruded on something. She felt like she walked in on a secret she could or would never fully comprehend.

The three walked around the neighborhood, stopping more times than usual. All the nosey old folks on the block wanted to talk to Alex. The occasional stops didn't bother Carmen and Sadira because it gave them more time to spend with Alex and learn about the stuff she seemed to gloss over whenever they asked. Alex, on the other hand, was annoyed. She was sick of answering all the same questions over and over again

'Girl, where you been? How's yo momma doin'? And that new rich doctor husband of hers? It must be nice to move away from this mess.'

"What mess are they talking about?" Carmen asked as they finally came to the end of the street, a block away from the park.

"Well, it is calmer and quieter in my neighborhood."

"Girl, this is your neighborhood," Sadira said.

Alex didn't feel like getting into it with Dee. She decided to just let it go. It was hard enough trying not to notice all the crushed cans, empty bottles, and various Jay's potato chip bags on the sidewalks. She didn't want to admit she was glad Carmen didn't want to stop at her house. She didn't know how she would react to the usually nasty house that would probably look worse to her after seeing how nice everyone's house was in her new neighborhood.

They made it to the park just in time for the end of South Side Academy's football team's practice. The three girls sat in the bleachers trying to act like they were not paying attention to the boy-men.

"Hey, shorty. Shorty in the red," boomed a male voice that interrupted their giggly gossip session.

"Who you talking to?" Carmen asked, reverting to her ghetto-tone smacking her lips and clicking her tongue. Her gum popped but she knew to whom they were talking. They were always talking to her. Guys didn't notice Alex and Sadira until Carmen picked out the one she wanted.

"I'm talking to you. You in the red."

"What you want?"

"Come here and holla at me."

"Whatever happened to them coming to us?" Alex asked.

"Girl you forgot where you are. This is the 'hood. You know boys gotta holla from across the way." Sadira replied.

By now Carmen had switched her hips over to the dark-skinned boy with a bald fade.

"Damn you thick," He said, complimenting her.

Carmen smiled, she knew there was a reason she put on her tight jeans, and these particular tight jeans were her booty jeans. They accentuated what her mother passed down to her. She slipped her acrylic tipped nails into her back pocket making her oversized breasts stick out even more than usual.

"What's your name?"

"Mike. You got a man?"

"Why?"

"Cuz I want to know."

"And if I do?"

"Then I would ask if you wanted a better one."

She giggled. "Let me get your number and I will tell you later."

"You got a pen?'

"Naw, but my girls do." She popped the gum in her mouth again before yelling, "One of ya'll got a pen or something?"

Sadira walked over to the two and pulled a pen out of her Coach skinny case.

"Hey," she said to him but felt like he didn't hear her because he towered over her 4'11" frame.

"Sup," he said to Carmen's breasts that got in the way of him seeing Sadira.

"I'm right here," she replied giving Carmen the pen and walking away.

"You babysitting?" He said writing his number and name on a gum wrapper Carmen handed him.

"Naw, that's my girl."

"She is so little, I just thought she was your lil' cousin or something."

"Naw, she's just petite."

Carmen was glad Sadira didn't hear that. She was always complaining about puberty never happening to her. Unlike her, Sadira lacked the thickness that Carmen possessed. But then again who would know what Sadira had because she wore her clothes two sizes too big. They swallowed her and made her look like she weighed less than her 108-pounds.

Two other guys stood behind Mike. Every once and a while Carmen would hear them laugh and heard the word ass being passed in their conversation like the football they tossed between them.

"I'll holla at you...," she looked at the paper, "Mike."

"Let me get your number too, just in case."

"Just in case what?"

"Just, just in case."

"Ok." Carmen only gave out her number if she really liked a boy.

It was hard to tell with Mike, he appeared to be on the good side of cute. But he was sweaty and hidden under his gear. He was tall and Carmen liked that, his baldness was a little sexy but she still didn't know if she would call him. She gave him her number and figured she'd leave the rest up to God.

"Are you gonna talk to him?" Sadira asked when Carmen came back switching a little harder this time because she knew the boys were watching her.

"She doesn't know," Alex answered.

"We'll see if he calls."

"I wish someone our age would talk to me."

"Dee, you have to start dressing like a girl," Alex said.

"Yeah Dee, the next time we go to the mall, let me pick you out something."

"Carmen, I don't want no titty shirt or booty pants."

"Hey, if you want the men…."

"That's not the only way to get men to talk to you," Alex said,

"You should come out to my house. It's a whole 'nother breed of brothas."

"I bet. This is the first time you talked about any men in your neighborhood. I thought there wasn't any."

"There's plenty I am finding out. My mom has joined The Links, so between reactivating with Jack and Jill chapter in HF and going to Links' functions with her I have met some people. It's hard trying not to talk about my new home at school. You know what will happen if too many people find out."

"Yeah," Carmen and Sadira nodded in agreement. Alex would be kicked out of the city public high school. Her living in Homewood-Flossmoor and going to school in the city was illegal unless of course, you had a hook up which is what Alex's stepfather had.

"I'll be glad when we all go to U of I next year, so we can do and talk about whatever the hell we want to," Sadira said.

"Yeah," the other two said, but deep down none of them were sure of what they would be doing next year.

Publisher's Note: *From a Black Perspective* is the beginning manifestation of several collective dreams. *Volume One, "The Blood,"* features five up-and-coming authors. As a whole, the project is a gathering of entertaining, inspirational, and educated voices modeled after the collective creative literary power of the long-celebrated Harlem Renaissance.

From a Black Perspective is a celebration of the diversity within the black literary community. It serves as an antithesis to the notion that the black community is monolithic in our interests, values, political views, and the genres in which we write but rather a people as varied as the hues of our skin. This three-part anthology affords Rainbow Room Publishing, LLC to fulfill one of its primary objectives: providing a vehicle and platform to facilitate the publication of as many diverse and otherwise underrepresented voices as possible.

Your support of this project further enables the publication of each contributing author's individual creative and publishing efforts while supporting numerous black voices. We invite you to embark with us on this three-part literary journey and encourage you to reserve space on your bookshelves for *Volume Two, "The People,"* highlighting more talented writers as well as more individual works from each of these published authors in 2021 and *Volume Three, "The Homeland"* in 2022.

Eddie S. Pierce
Founder & Publisher
Rainbow Room Publishing

For more information on Rainbow Room Publishing, LLC, our products and services visit:

www.rainbowroompublishing.com

Made in the USA
Coppell, TX
28 May 2021